Debbie mumm's®

CUDDLE QUILTS

FOR LITTLE GIRLS AND BOYS

Nothing is more exciting or challenging than welcoming little ones to our lives! Get ready for the heartwarming, hilarious, hardworking, and hugely rewarding times that come with kids by creating colorful and fun-loving quilts and decor for nurseries and toddler rooms.

Dear Friends,

Babies and little ones have a way of making hearts melt. When a new baby joins the family, it is such a joy to plan a cuddly quilt or projects for the entire nursery. A new baby gives Mom, Grandma, and all the aunties (official and unofficial) just the inspiration they are looking for to make a fun totebag for mom, frames for sweet photos, a decorative wallhanging, or cuddly crib quilt. And, when baby outgrows the nursery, you'll find lots of ideas for rooms that are sure to please the little girls and boys in your life.

Debbie with Kate, 1 year old

Since little girls are so passionate about pink and purple we couldn't resist those girl-crazy colors in a fun assortment of bed quilts, a headboard, and bedside lamps (naturally you can adapt to any color scheme!). Sugar and spice themes like butterflies, hearts, and flowers are sure-fire to win over the heart of your favorite little girl. Growing boys gravitate towards snips and snails, cars and trucks, frogs and boats. Encourage that boundless energy when you fill his room with bright and primary colors, with a clever room organizer, playful twin bed quilt, and a painted toy chest.

This book is all about sewing and decorating for the exciting experience of having a child in your life. And since time moves particularly fast when children are young, projects in this book are designed to be quick, easy and fun!

Release your inner child, and cuddle up the kids by creating quilts, crafts, and décor for the special little ones in your life.

Enjoy this special time,

Debbie Mumm

TABLE OF CONTENTS

Baby Love

Moon & Stars Crib Quilt 6

Moon & Stars Twin Quilt 8

Brightest Star Wall Art 10

Moon & Stars Mobile 11

Zigzag Zoo Crib Quilt 12

Zigzag Zoo Twin Quilt 14

Zigzag Zoo Notebook..............................15

Zigzag Zoo Tote Bag 17

Silly Safari Wall Quilt 18

Silly Safari Crib Quilt...............................24

Silly Safari Twin Quilt 26

Silly Safari Wheelies 26

Lion Pillow 27

Baby Blooms Crib Quilt 28

Baby Blooms Window Valance 32

Blooming Hat Boxes 33

Baby Blooms Growth Chart 34

Girly Girls

Flutterby Twin Quilt................................38

Flutterby Crib Quilt.................................40

Flutterby Pillow Sham 42

Name in Frames......................................43

Butterfly Bling...44

Girl Stuff...45

Flutterby Headboard...............................46

Butterfly Photo Holder 47

Sugar & Spice Twin Bed Quilt 48

Everything Nice Wall Quilt 54

Sugar & Spice Pillow................................56

Sugar & Spice Lamp 57

All Boy

Road Rally Twin Bed Quilt 60

Road Rally Letters 63

Let's Go Organizer...................................64

Beep Beep Toy Chest...............................69

Road Rally Pillow Sham............................70

Road Rally Lamp 71

Snips & Snails Wall or Crib Quilt 72

Snips & Snails Twin Bed Quilt 78

Snips & Snails Drawer Pulls 83

Snips & Snails Window Valance 84

Polka Dot Pegs..85

Frog Pillow..86

Collector Jars 88

Frog Wall Art...89

Cute Critters Wall Art..............................90

Other Stuff

About This Book...................................... 2

General Directions 92

About Debbie...96

Credits 96

BABY LOVE

SWEET LITTLE ONES FIND JOYS IN CUTE ANIMALS, CUDDLY BLANKIES, AND BABY TOYS.

Gavin - 6 Months Old

Enjoy the sound of sweet baby laughter as you tuck your little one under a cozy handmade quilt. Choose your favorite cuddly theme to create the perfect place for your little love.

Dylan - 6 Months Old

MOON & STARS CRIB QUILT

Making the Patchwork Blocks

1. Sew lengthwise one 6" x 42" Fabric C strip between one 3" x 42" Fabric A strip, and one 4½" Fabric B strip as shown. Press. Make two. Cut strip sets into twelve 4"-wide segments as shown.

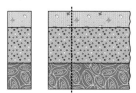

4

Make 2
Cut 12 segments

2. Sew lengthwise one 6" x 42" Fabric A strip between one 4½" x 42" Fabric B strip, and one 3" Fabric D strip as shown. Press. Make two. Cut strip sets into twelve 5½"-wide segments as shown.

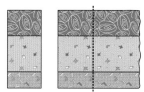

5½

Make 2
Cut 12 segments

3. Sew lengthwise one 3" x 42" Fabric D strip between one 4" x 42" Fabric C strip, and one 6½" Fabric E strip as shown. Press. Make two. Cut strip sets into twelve 4"-wide segments as shown.

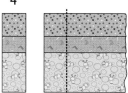

4

Make 2
Cut 12 segments

Moon & Stars Crib Quilt Finished Size: 45" x 57"	FIRST CUT		SECOND CUT	
	Number of Strips or Pieces	Dimensions	Number of Pieces	Dimensions
Fabric A Background ⅝ yard	2 2	6" x 42" 3" x 42"		
Fabric B Background ⅝ yard	4	4½" x 42"		
Fabric C Background ⅝ yard	2 2	6" x 42" 4" x 42"		
Fabric D Background ½ yard	4	3" x 42"		
Fabric E Background ½ yard	2	6½" x 42"		
First Border ⅓ yard	5	1½" x 42"	2	1½" x 36½"
Outside Border ⅝ yard	5	3½" x 42"	2	3½" x 38½"
Binding ⅝ yard	6	2¾" x 42"		
Moon Appliqués - ⅜ yard Star Appliqués - ¼ yard Backing - 2⅞ yards Batting - 50" x 63" Lightweight Fusible Web - 1 yard				

Fabric Requirements and Cutting Instructions

Read all instructions before beginning and use ¼"-wide seam allowances throughout. Read Cutting Strips and Pieces on page 92 prior to cutting fabric.

Getting Started

These moons and stars shine brightly, illuminating our patchwork night sky. Blocks measure 12½" square (unfinished). Refer to Accurate Seam Allowance on page 92. Whenever possible use the Assembly Line Method on page 92. Press seams in the direction of arrows.

4. Sew one segment from step 2 between one segment from step 1 and one segment from step 3 as shown. Press. Make twelve. Block measures 12½" square.

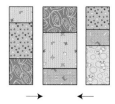

→   ←

Make 12
Block measures 12½" square

5. Refer to layout on page 8 noting orientation of blocks. Arrange and sew four rows with three blocks each. Press seams in opposite directions from row to row. Sew rows together. Press.

Adding the Appliqués

Refer to appliqué instructions on page 93. Our instructions are for Quick-Fuse Appliqué, but if you prefer hand appliqué, reverse templates and add ¼"-wide seam allowances.

1. Use patterns on page 9 to trace three moons, three large stars and six small stars on paper side of fusible web. Use appropriate fabrics to prepare all appliqués for fusing.

2. Refer to layout on page 8 to position and fuse appliqués to quilt. Finish appliqué edges with machine satin stitch or other decorative stitching as desired.

MOON & STARS CRIB QUILT
Finished Size: 45" x 57"

Stars and moons will light baby's way to Dreamland when he's tucked under this snuggly quilt. Strip piecing makes the background super easy and there's no seam matching within blocks. Lustrous minky moon appliqués add shine and even more softness to this charming quilt.

Adding the Borders

1. Refer to Adding the Borders on page 94. Sew two 1½" x 36½" First Border strips to top and bottom of quilt. Press seams toward border.

2. Sew remaining 1½" x 42" First Border strips together end-to-end to make one continuous 1½"-wide First Border strip. Measure quilt through center from top to bottom. Cut two 1½"-wide First Border strips to this measurement. Sew to sides of quilt. Press.

3. Sew two 3½" x 38½" Outside Border strips to top and bottom of quilt. Press seams toward border.

4. Refer to step 2 to join, measure, trim, and sew remaining 3½"-wide Outside Border strips to sides of quilt. Press.

Layering and Finishing

1. Cut backing crosswise into two equal pieces. Sew pieces together lengthwise to make one 51" x 80" (approximate) backing piece. Press and trim to 51" x 63".

2. Referring to Layering the Quilt on page 94, arrange and baste backing, batting, and top together. Hand or machine quilt as desired.

3. Refer to Binding the Quilt on page 94. Sew 2¾" x 42" binding strips end-to-end to make one continuous 2¾"-wide binding strip. Press. Bind quilt to finish.

MOON & STARS CRIB QUILT
Finished Size: 45" x 57"

Moon & Stars Twin Bed Quilt	FIRST CUT	
Finished Size: 69" x 81" 30 Blocks 5 across by 6 down	Number of Strips or Pieces	Dimensions
Fabric A Background 1¼ yards	5 3	6" x 42" 3" x 42"
Fabric B Background 1⅛ yards	8	4½" x 42"
Fabric C Background 1 yard	3 3	6" x 42" 4" x 42"
Fabric D Background ⅞ yard	8	3" x 42"
Fabric E Background ⅝ yard	3	6½" x 42"
First Border ⅜ yard	7	1½" x 42"
Outside Border 1 yard	8	3½" x 42"
Binding ¾ yard	8	2¾" x 42"
Backing - 5 yards Batting - 76" x 88"		

MAKE IT TWIN SIZE

For Twin Size Quilt, follow directions for block construction, making three strip sets for steps 1 and 3 and five strip sets for step 2. Cut thirty segments from strip sets in each step. Make thirty blocks. Adjust appliqué fabric and lightweight fusible web for number of stars and moons desired. Assemble six rows of five blocks each and add borders.

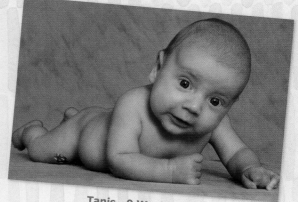

Tanis - 9 Weeks Old

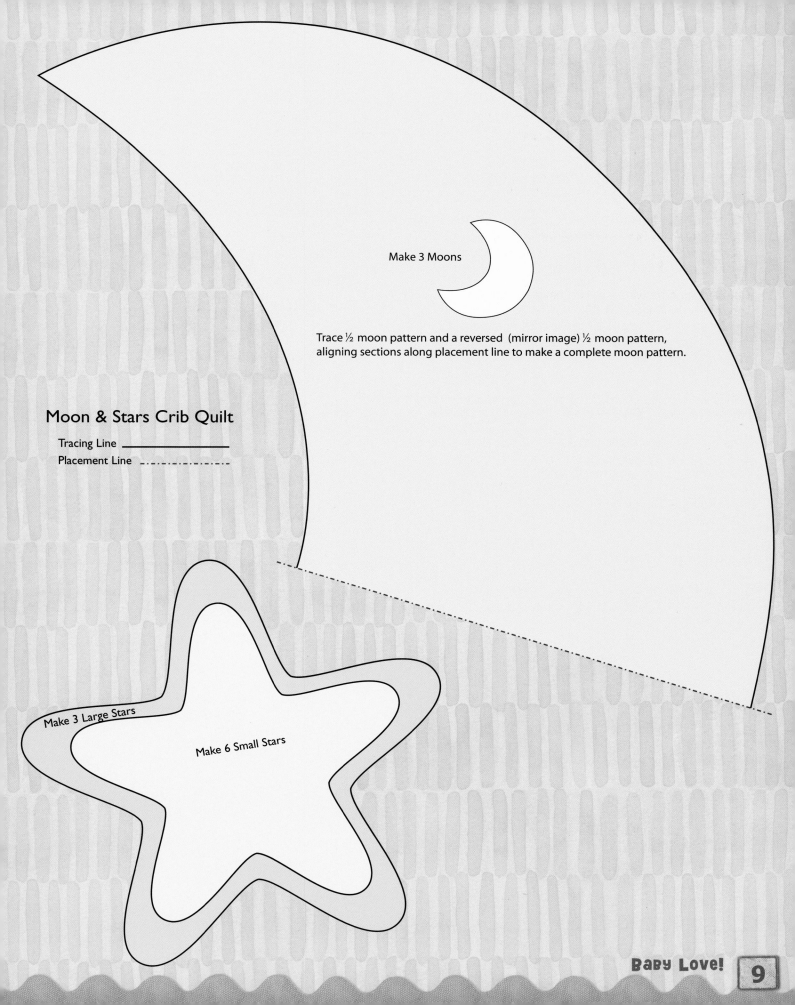

Make 3 Moons

Trace ½ moon pattern and a reversed (mirror image) ½ moon pattern, aligning sections along placement line to make a complete moon pattern.

Moon & Stars Crib Quilt

Tracing Line _____

Placement Line _ _ _ _ _ _ _

Make 3 Large Stars

Make 6 Small Stars

BRIGHTEST STAR
WALL ART

1. Refer to General Painting Directions on page 95. Apply Gesso to MDF board and allow to dry completely. Lightly sand for a smooth surface and remove residue with cloth.

2. Mix Wedgwood Blue with White paint to make a very light blue. Apply paint to prepared board. Two or more coats of paint may be needed for good coverage. Always allow paint to dry thoroughly after each coat.

3. Mix Wedgwood Blue with White paint to make a blue about two shades darker than base coat. Using check stencil and sponge, stencil checks onto board. Dip sponge in paint color, blot several times on a paper towel, then using an up and down motion, apply paint to stencil. Carefully remove stencil. Allow to dry thoroughly.

4. Lightly sand painted surface to blur edges and soften checks. Remove sanding residue with cloth.

5. Decide placement of poem on board. Cut apart each line and adjust as needed, being careful that ascenders and descenders do not overlap. Use a T-square to level each line, peel back paper and use the tool provided to adhere the vinyl letters to prepared board—a quick solution with a hand-painted look. Apply matte varnish to plaque.

6. If tin stars and moon have a rust finish, sand well and remove residue with cloth. Paint with Gesso or use a spray primer and allow to dry. Apply Moon Yellow to stars and moon. Two or more coats may be needed for good coverage. Allow paint to dry thoroughly after each coat.

SUPPLIES

12" x 24" MDF (Medium-Density Fiberboard)

Gesso

Acrylic Craft Paint — **Delta Ceramcoat®** **White and Wedgwood Blue;** **Americana® Moon Yellow**

Assorted Paintbrushes

Matte Varnish

Stencil with 1½" Checks

Stencil Sponge

Fine Sandpaper

Two Tin Stars and Tin Moon

Ultra-Fine Yellow Glitter

Star Beads

Foam Mounting Tape

Craft Glue

T-Square

Vinyl Words*
We ordered our vinyl words from www.quotethewalls.com. There are many poems and phrases to select from or you can customize a poem, saying, or words to suit your décor. Vinyl words can be used directly on a wall, but we chose to make a plaque for a permanent keepsake.

7. Apply matte varnish to stars and moon. While varnish is wet, sprinkle with yellow glitter. Allow to dry. Use foam mounting tape to adhere stars and moon to plaque. Glue on star beads to dot each "i" and to accent the moon.

As sweet as baby... declare your love with this wall plaque that's certain to be the centerpiece of the nursery. An easy shortcut makes creating this plaque surprisingly simple. Glittery stars and a moon add sparkle to this tender tribute.

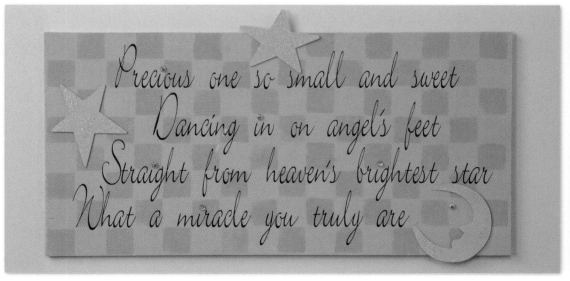

Precious one so small and sweet
Dancing in on angel's feet
Straight from heaven's brightest star
What a miracle you truly are

Moon & Stars
MOBILE

Glittery stars and moon and gleaming beads are sure to catch baby's attention and to catch the eyes of all visitors to the nursery. This easy mobile moves with air currents and adds a darling decoration to unused space near the ceiling. Hang the mobile high and keep out of reach of all children. Visit a Christmas store for star possibilities.

Making the Mobile

1. Referring to photo, drill one hole in top of large star, if needed, holes in two bottom points of large star, top and bottom of moon, top point and center point of one small star, and top point of two stars. Holes should be large enough to insert cord. Remove residue with damp cloth.

2. Paint stars and moon with Moon Yellow paint. Two or more coats of paint may be needed for good coverage. Paint one side at a time and allow to dry completely after each coat.

3. Mix small amount of Burnt Umber paint with Clear Glaze using a 1:5 ratio. Apply mixed glaze to edges of each star and moon to add shadows and dimension. Do one side at a time and use a damp cloth to wipe off excess glaze.

4. Apply varnish to stars and moon and sprinkle edges with glitter while varnish is still wet. Do one side at a time and allow to dry thoroughly.

5. Using photo for inspiration, string beads as desired on cord and tie to stars and moon to string mobile together tying knots as needed. Do not trim excess cord at this point. Tie cord to top of star to hang.

6. When mobile is complete, put a drop of clear glue on each knot and allow to dry. Trim off excess cord and hang mobile as desired.

SUPPLIES

Large Papier-Mâché Star

Three Dimensional Stars
(4"-5" point to point)

Tin or Wooden Moon
(approximately 4¼" diameter)

Assorted Blue Beads with Large Holes

¼" Faceted Yellow Beads

.039 Yellow Leather Cord
(Found with jewelry supplies)

Acrylic Craft Paint - Americana® Moon Yellow; Delta Ceramcoat® Burnt Umber

Clear Glaze

Matte Varnish

Assorted Paintbrushes

UltraFine Glitter in a Gold/Copper Mix

Drill and Small Bit

Clear Craft Glue

Tack Cloth

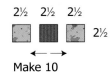

ZIGZAG ZOO
CRIB QUILT

Zigzag Zoo Crib Quilt Finished Size: 50" x 60"	FIRST CUT		SECOND CUT	
	Number of Strips or Pieces	Dimensions	Number of Pieces	Dimensions
Fabric A Block 1 Center ⅛ yard	1	2½" x 42"	10	2½" squares
Fabric B Block 1 Background ½ yard	5	2½" x 42"	20 20	2½" x 6½" 2½" squares
Fabric C Block 2 Center ½ yard	2	6½" x 42"	10	6½" squares
Fabric D Block Border Dark 1 yard	12	2½" x 42"	20 20 20	2½" x 10½" 2½" x 6½" 2½" squares
Fabric E Block Border Light 1 yard	12	2½" x 42"	20 20 20	2½" x 10½" 2½" x 6½" 2½" squares
Accent Border ¼ yard	5	1" x 42"		
Outside Border 1 yard	6	4½" x 42"		
Binding ⅝ yard	6	2¾" x 42"		
Backing - 3⅛ yards Batting - 56" x 66"				

Fabric Requirements and Cutting Instructions

Read all instructions before beginning and use ¼"-wide seam allowances throughout. Read Cutting Strips and Pieces on page 92 prior to cutting fabric.

Getting Started

Fun and colorful animal print fabrics take center stage in this playful quilt. Blocks measure 10½" square (unfinished). Refer to Accurate Seam Allowance on page 92. Whenever possible use the Assembly Line Method on page 92. Press seams in the direction of arrows.

Making the Blocks

1. Sew one 2½" Fabric A square between two 2½" Fabric B squares as shown. Press. Make ten.

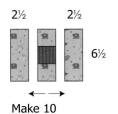

Make 10

2. Sew one unit from step 1 between two 2½" x 6½" Fabric B pieces as shown. Press. Make ten.

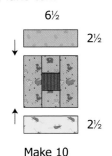

Make 10

3. Sew one unit from step 2 between one 2½" x 6½" Fabric D piece and one 2½" x 6½" Fabric E piece as shown. Press. Make ten.

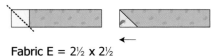

Make 10

4. Refer to Quick Corner Triangles on page 92. Making a quick corner triangle unit, sew one 2½" Fabric E square to one 2½" x 10½" Fabric D piece. Press. Make twenty.

Fabric E = 2½ x 2½
Fabric D = 2½ x 10½
Make 20

5. Making a quick corner triangle unit, sew one 2½" Fabric D square to one 2½" x 10½" Fabric E piece as shown. Press. Make twenty.

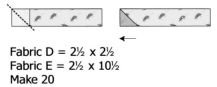

Fabric D = 2½ x 2½
Fabric E = 2½ x 10½
Make 20

6. Sew one unit from step 3 between one unit from step 4 and one unit from step 5 as shown. Press. Make ten and label Block 1. Block measures 10½" square.

Block 1

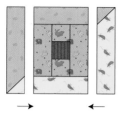

→   ←

Make 10
Block measures 10½" square

7. Sew one 6½" Fabric C square between one 2½" x 6½" Fabric D piece and one 2½" x 6½" Fabric E piece as shown. Press. Make ten.

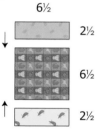

6½

2½

6½

2½

Make 10

8. Sew one unit from step 7 between one unit from step 4 and one unit from step 5 as shown. Press. Make ten and label Block 2. Block measures 10½" square.

Block 2

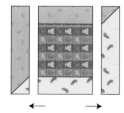

←   →

Make 10
Block measures 10½" square

ZIGZAG ZOO CRIB QUILT
Finished Size: 50" x 60"

Bright colors zigzag across this eye-catching quilt creating the illusion of a diagonal pattern. This quilt is perfect for showing off a favorite panel fabric or a strong pattern. Baby and parents will love this bright and beautiful quilt.

Assembly the Quilt

1. Refer to layout to sew together five rows with four blocks each, alternating Block 1 and Block 2 placement from row to row. Press rows in opposite direction from row to row.

2. Arrange and sew rows together. Press.

3. Refer to Adding the Borders on page 94. Sew 1" x 42" Accent Border strips together end-to-end to make one continuous 1"-wide Accent Border strip. Measure quilt through center from side to side. Cut two 1"-wide Accent Border strips to this measurement. Sew to top and bottom of quilt. Press seams toward border.

4. Measure quilt through center from top to bottom including border just added. Cut two 1"-wide Accent Border strips to this measurement. Sew to sides of quilt. Press.

5. Refer to steps 3 and 4 to join, measure, trim, and sew 4½"-wide Outside Border strips to top, bottom, and sides of quilt. Press.

Layering and Finishing

1. Cut backing crosswise into two equal pieces. Sew pieces together lengthwise to make one 56" x 80" (approximate) backing piece. Press and trim to 56" x 66".

2. Referring to Layering the Quilt on page 94, arrange and baste backing, batting, and top together. Hand or machine quilt as desired.

3. Refer to Binding the Quilt on page 94. Sew 2¾" x 42" binding strips end-to-end to make one continuous 2¾"-wide binding strip. Bind quilt to finish.

ZIGZAG ZOO CRIB QUILT
· Finished Size: 50" x 60" ·

Gavin - 6 Months Old

MAKE IT TWIN SIZE

To make the Twin Quilt, you will make 35 blocks. Eighteen of Block 1 and seventeen of Block 2. Follow directions for block construction. To assemble quilt, sew seven rows of five blocks each.

Zigzag Zoo Twin Bed Quilt Finished Size: 60" x 80" 35 Blocks 5 across by 7 down	FIRST CUT		SECOND CUT	
	Number of Strips or Pieces	Dimensions	Number of Pieces	Dimensions
Fabric A Block 1 Center ¼ yard	2	2½" x 42"	18	2½" squares
Fabric B Block 1 Background ¾ yard	9	2½" x 42"	36 36	2½" x 6½" 2½" squares
Fabric C Block 2 Center ⅝ yard	3	6½" x 42"	17	6½" squares
Fabric D Block Border Dark 1⅝ yards	21	2½" x 42"	35 35 35	2½" x 10½" 2½" x 6½" 2½" squares
Fabric E Block Border Light 1⅝ yards	21	2½" x 42"	35 35 35	2½" x 10½" 2½" x 6½" 2½" squares
Accent Border ¼ yard	7	1" x 42"		
Outside Border 1 yard	7	4½" x 42"		
Binding ⅔ yard	8	2¾" x 42"		
Backing - 5 yards Batting - 68" x 88"				

Zigzag Zoo
NOTEBOOK

This quick and cute gift idea is sure to be a hit with a new mom! A small spiral-bound notebook is personalized with cute cut-outs and scrapbook products to create a handy reference for lists, baby notes, and sitter information.

Embellishing the Notebook

1. Cut green cardstock to size of notebook cover excluding wire binding area.

2. Cut yellow scrapbook paper an ⅛" smaller on top, bottom and right side than green paper just cut. Left side should be ¼" smaller than green paper.

3. Cut blue cardstock to 2" x 7½".

4. Following manufacturer's directions, iron fusible web to back of fabric scrap. Select icons to be featured and "fussy-cut" pieces. Position and iron fabric to blue cardstock.

5. Following package directions, apply zigzag rub-on stitches around each fabric piece.

6. Position and glue embellished blue cardstock to yellow scrapbook paper, leaving room for rub-on letters.

7. Use rub-on letters to write Mom Notes or personalize with a name. Apply rub-on stitches as a border on yellow scrapbook paper.

8. Glue embellished yellow scrapbook paper to green cardstock, offsetting it ¼" on left side and ⅛" on top, bottom, and right side. Glue green cardstock to notebook cover.

9. Glue rickrack on left side of cover as shown, wrapping ends to the inside and gluing firmly.

Small Wire-Bound Notebook (4" x 8½")

Green and Blue Cardstock — Scraps

Yellow Scrapbook Paper — Scrap

Rub-on Letters and Stitches

Blue Rickrack — Scrap

Fabric Scrap to Match Tote

Lightweight Fusible Web

Clear Scrapbook Glue

*Debbie Mumm® scrapbook products are available at Jo-Ann Fabric and Craft Stores.

ZigZag Zoo
TOTE BAG

Zigzag Zoo Tote Bag Finished Size: 18" x 15"	FIRST CUT	
	Number of Strips or Pieces	Dimensions
Fabric A Tote & Clousure Tab ½ yard	1	12½" x 37"
	1	2½" x 4"
Fabric B Pocket & Band Accent ⅝ yard	1	15½" x 37"
	1	3½" x 37"
Fabric C Handles, Closure Tab & Lining 1⅛ yards	1	16" x 37"
	4	4½" x 42"
	1	4½" x 5"
	2	1½" x 5"
	1	1½" x 2½"
Batting - One 18" x 42" (Tote) One 8" x 38" (Pocket) Four 1½" x 66" (Handles) Four 5" x 6" (Tab) Backing - 18" x 42" muslin (will not show) 1" Button - 5 Hook and Loop tape - ⅛ yard or desired closure		

Getting Started

Every good zookeeper needs a tote of toys and supplies! Read all instructions before beginning this project. Note this project uses both ½"-wide and ¼"-wide seam allowances. Press seams in the direction of arrows.

Making the Tote

1. Using a ¼"-wide seam allowance, sew one 3½" x 37" Fabric B strip to one 12½" x 37" Fabric A piece as shown. Press.

37

3½

12½

2. Place unit from step 1 on 18" x 42" batting and backing pieces and quilt as desired. Trim batting and backing even with tote edges. Top stitch bottom edge of accent band.

3. Fold 15½" x 37" Fabric B piece lengthwise right sides together. Place folded piece on 8" x 38" batting and using ¼"-wide seam, sew along length of pocket only. Trim batting close to stitching, even with pocket edges and close to folded edge of pocket. Trim backing. Clip corners, turn, and press. Top stitch ¼" away from top edge only. Add additional quilting as desired.

4. Referring to diagram below, arrange and pin pocket to unit from step 2, 3½" from bottom edge as shown. Top stitch ¼" away from pocket bottom edge. Baste side edges in place.

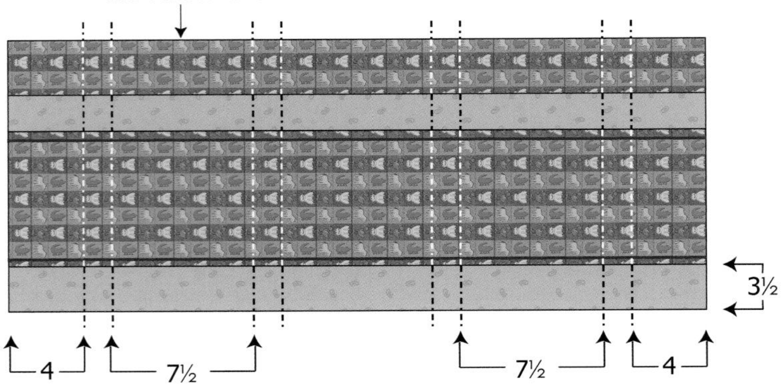

Tab Placement

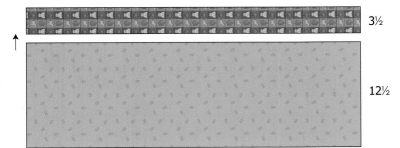

3½

4 — 7½ — 7½ — 4

5. Sew two 4½" x 42" Fabric C strips together end-to-end to make one continuous 4½"-wide Fabric C strip. Press. Make two. Cut strip into two 4½" x 66" lengths for handles.

6. Fold under one long side of handle strip ¼" to wrong side. Press. Fold and press under opposite side 1¼". Repeat for other handle strip.

7. Center two layers of batting on wrong side of one strip from step 6. Fold 1¼" edge over batting, and then fold ¼" edge over, covering fabric. Press. Stitch close to folded edges. Repeat for other handle strip.

8. Determine desired length of handle, and cut handles to this length. Note. Our handles were cut to 61". Refer to diagram in step 4, and photo below, for handle placement. Position and pin handles 4" from outside edge and 7½" apart as shown. Top stitch handles to tote, stopping 1" from top edge. (Handles will be reinforced after lining is sewn in place.)

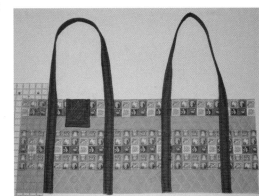

9. Sew one 2½" x 4" Fabric A piece to one 1½" x 2½" Fabric C piece. Press seam toward Fabric C. Sew this unit between two 1½" x 5" Fabric C pieces as shown. Press.

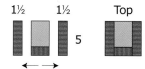

10. Layer and center unit from step 9 and 4" x 5" backing piece right sides together on 5" x 6" batting; wrong side of backing on 5" x 6" batting piece. Using ¼"-wide seam, stitch two sides and bottom, leaving top free of stitching. Trim batting close to stitching and backing even with unit edges. Clip corners, turn, and press. Quilt as desired.

11. Referring to step 8 photo and step 4 diagram, center tab closure unit from step 10 to tote between one set of handles as shown. Stitch using ¼"-wide seam.

Finishing the Tote

1. Fold tote unit, right sides together, in half crosswise to make an 18½" x 15½" folded unit. Sew along side and bottom edges, using ½"-wide seam. Press seam open.

2. Fold one bottom corner of unit from step 1, matching side seam to bottom seam. Draw a 4"-long line across as shown. Sew on drawn line, anchoring stitches. Repeat for other corner.

3. Fold stitched corners to bottom seam of tote and tack in place for added stability.

4. Using 16" x 37" Lining piece, repeat steps 1-3 to make lining insert. Leave a 5" opening along side seam for turning.

5. Turn tote wrong side out. Position and pin lining inside tote, right sides together, making sure tab is between layers and handles are free. Stitch lining and tote together along top edge using a ¼"-wide seam allowance. Turn right side out and press leaving ¼" of lining showing on front side of tote. "Stitch-in-the-ditch" along seam line of tote and lining, to hold lining in place.

ZIGZAG ZOO TOTE BAG
Finished Size: 18" x 15"

Fun and functional, with this diaper bag you can take a touch of the nursery décor with you wherever you go. Quilted for strength, with lots of useful pockets, and a deep interior, this tote is as useful as it is cute.

6. Referring to photo below add reinforcing stitches to handles. Sew hook and loop tape to tab and tote to create tote closure or use closure of your choice. Stitch decorative button to tab section and at intersections where handles meet top edge of pocket.

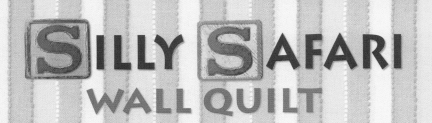

Silly Safari Wall Quilt

Silly Safari Wall Quilt Finished Size: 38" x 24½"	FIRST CUT		SECOND CUT	
	Number of Strips or Pieces	Dimensions	Number of Pieces	Dimensions
Fabric A Rail Fence Blocks ⅛ yard each of eight fabrics	1*	1½" x 42" *cut for each fabric		
Fabric B Elephant & Giraffe Background ⅓ yard	1	8½" x 42"	1 1	8½" x 16½" 8½" square
Fabric C Lion Background ⅓ yard	1	8½" square		
Fabric D Zebra Background ⅓ yard	1	8½" square		
Fabric E Grass ⅛ yard	1	2½" x 42"	2	2½" x 8½"
First Border ⅙ yard	3	1" x 42"	2 2	1" x 32½" 1" x 17½"
Second Border ⅙ yard	1 2	1½" x 42" 1" x 42"	1 1 2	1½" x 33½" 1" x 33½" 1" x 19"
Outside Border ⅓ yard	1 2	3½" x 42" 2½" x 42"	1 1 2	3½" x 38½" 2½" x 38½" 2½" x 19"

Animal Appliqués - Assorted Scraps
Backing - ⅞ yard
Batting - 27½" x 42"
Lightweight Fusible Web - ¾ yard
Buttons - 5
Rickrack Trim - 1 yard each in 2 colors

Optional Trims
Embroidery Floss
Beads - animal eyes
Fleece - scrap

Fabric Requirements and Cutting Instructions

Read all instructions before beginning and use ¼"-wide seam allowances throughout. Read Cutting Strips and Pieces on page 92 prior to cutting fabric.

Getting Started

Create an African Adventurer's theme by making and displaying this safari wall quilt in a room accented with the crib quilt on page 24. Refer to Accurate Seam Allowance on page 92. Whenever possible use the Assembly Line Method on page 92. Press seams in the direction of arrows.

Making the Safari Rail Fence Blocks

1. Sew together lengthwise four 1½" x 42" assorted Fabric A strips. Press. Cut strip set into six 4½"-wide segments as shown.

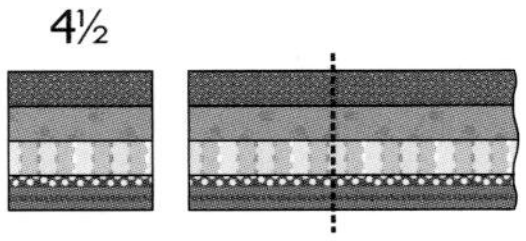

Cut 6 segments

2. Sew together lengthwise the remaining four 1½" x 42" assorted Fabric A strips. Press. Cut strip set into six 4½"-wide segments as shown.

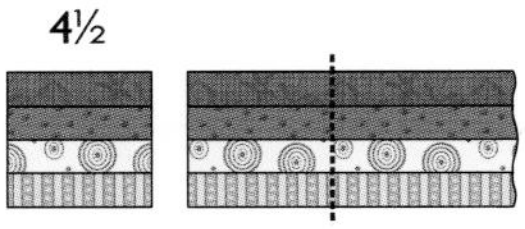

Cut 6 segments

3. Sew one unit from step 1 and one unit from step 2 together as shown. Press. Make six, three of each variation and combination.

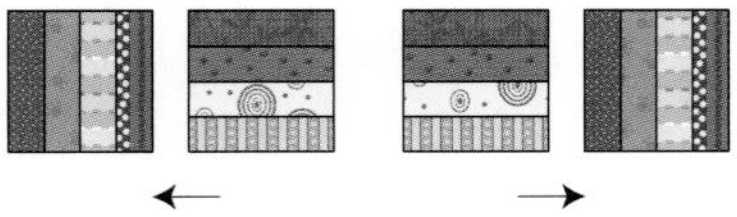
Make 3 Make 3

4. Sew two units from step 3, one of each variation, together as shown. Refer to Twisting Seams on page 92. Press. Make three. Block measures 8½" square.

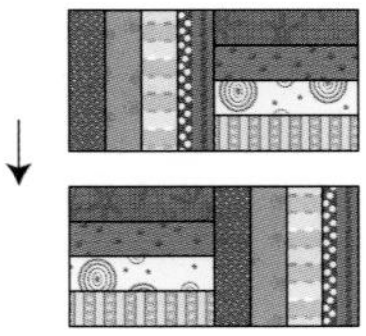
Make 3
Block measures 8½" square

SILLY SAFARI WALL QUILT
Finished Size: 38" x 24½"

Baby will go wild for these lovable animal characters! Dots and stripes and paw prints will catch baby's eye and dimensional trims will make these jungle animals even more endearing. Simple rail fence blocks enclose these sweet appliquéd animals.

Making the Animal Blocks

Refer to appliqué instructions on page 93. Our instructions are for Quick-Fuse Appliqué, but if you prefer hand appliqué, reverse templates and add ¼"-wide seam allowances. For steps 2-9 refer to photo prior to fusing appliqués to blocks. APPLIQUÉ NOTE: For lion mane we used a 1¼" strip of clipped fleece and inserted it under the lion head before stitching around head. For giraffe, we used a wide piece of rickrack behind the head and body for the mane. For the zebra, we use a piece of clipped wool and inserted it under the head and body before stitching. We used beads for eyes, French knots for giraffe nostrils and embroidered mouth for lion.

1. Use patterns on pages 20-23 to trace elephant, lion, giraffe, sun, and zebra on paper side of fusible web. Use appropriate fabrics to prepare all appliqués for fusing.

2. Trace elephant ear on page 21 on pattern paper or template plastic. Cut on drawn line. Trace four ears on wrong side of fabric piece. Cut on drawn line.

3. Place two ears right sides together. Stitch using ¼"-wide seam around outside curve only, leaving inside curve free of stitching for turning. Clip curve, turn right side out, and press. Take a small tuck in center of raw edge to add dimension, and baste in place. Repeat for other ear.

4. Refer to elephant pattern ear placement lines on page 21, arrange and fuse elephant to 8½" Fabric B square placing one ear unit from step 3 between head and body pieces and one ear unit between head and Fabric B background square. Finish appliqué edges with machine satin stitch or other decorative stitching as desired.

5. Using pinking shears or wavy rotary cutter trim one 8½" side of 2½" x 8½" Fabric E piece. Make two grass units. Place one grass unit on 8½" Fabric C square, aligning raw edges, and placing pinked edge in towards center. Stitch grass in place by topstitching just below pinked edge. Repeat step to arrange and stitch grass unit to 8½" x 16½" Fabric B piece.

6. Refer to photo to position and fuse lion to 8½" unit from step 5. Finish appliqué edges with machine satin stitch or other decorative stitching as desired.

7. Position and fuse giraffe and sun pieces to 8½" x 16½" unit from step 5. Finish appliqué edges with machine satin stitch or other decorative stitching as desired.

8. Position and fuse zebra to 8½" Fabric D square. Finish appliqué edges with machine satin stitch or other decorative stitching as desired.

Assembly

1. Referring to photo on page 19, arrange and sew one Rail Fence block to one 8½" animal block. Press seam toward Rail Fence block. Make three, one of each 8½" animal block square.

2. Referring to photo on page 19, arrange and sew lion and elephant units from step 1 together. Press.

3. Referring to photo on page 19, arrange and sew one giraffe block to one zebra unit from step 1. Press. Sew unit from step 2 to this unit. Press.

4. Sew unit from step 3 between two 1" x 32½" First Border strips. Press toward border. Sew two 1" x 17½" First Border strips to sides. Press.

5. Sew unit from step 4 between one 1" x 33½" (top edge) and 1½" x 33½" (bottom edge) Second Border strips. Press seams toward border just sewn. Sew two 1" x 19" Second Border strips to sides. Press.

6. Refer to photo on page 19 to layer and sew rickrack to bottom Second Border strip. Keep trim free of bottom seam allowance.

7. Sew unit between two 2½" x 19" (side edge) Outside Border strips. Press seams toward border just sewn.

8. Sew unit between one 2½" x 38½" (top edge) Outside Border strip and one 3½" x 38½" (bottom edge) Outside Border strip. Press.

Layering and Finishing

1. Layer and center top and backing, right sides together, on batting, wrong side of backing on batting. Using ¼"-wide seam, stitch around all edges, leaving a 6" opening for turning. Trim batting close to stitching and backing even with edges. Clip corners, turn, and press. Hand-stitch opening closed.

2. Machine or hand quilt as desired. Add beads, buttons, and other embellishments as desired.

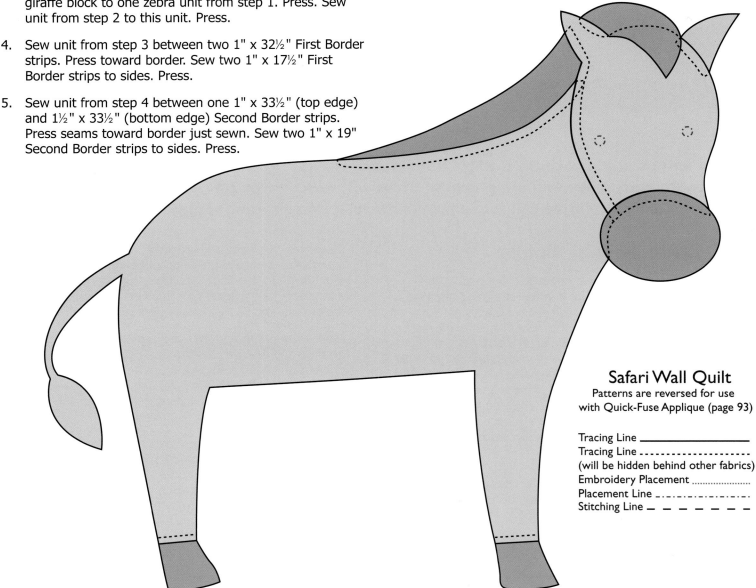

Safari Wall Quilt
Patterns are reversed for use with Quick-Fuse Applique (page 93)

Tracing Line _____
Tracing Line - - - - - - - - - - -
(will be hidden behind other fabrics)
Embroidery Placement ....
Placement Line _ . _ . _ . _ . _ . _ .
Stitching Line _ _ _ _ _ _ _

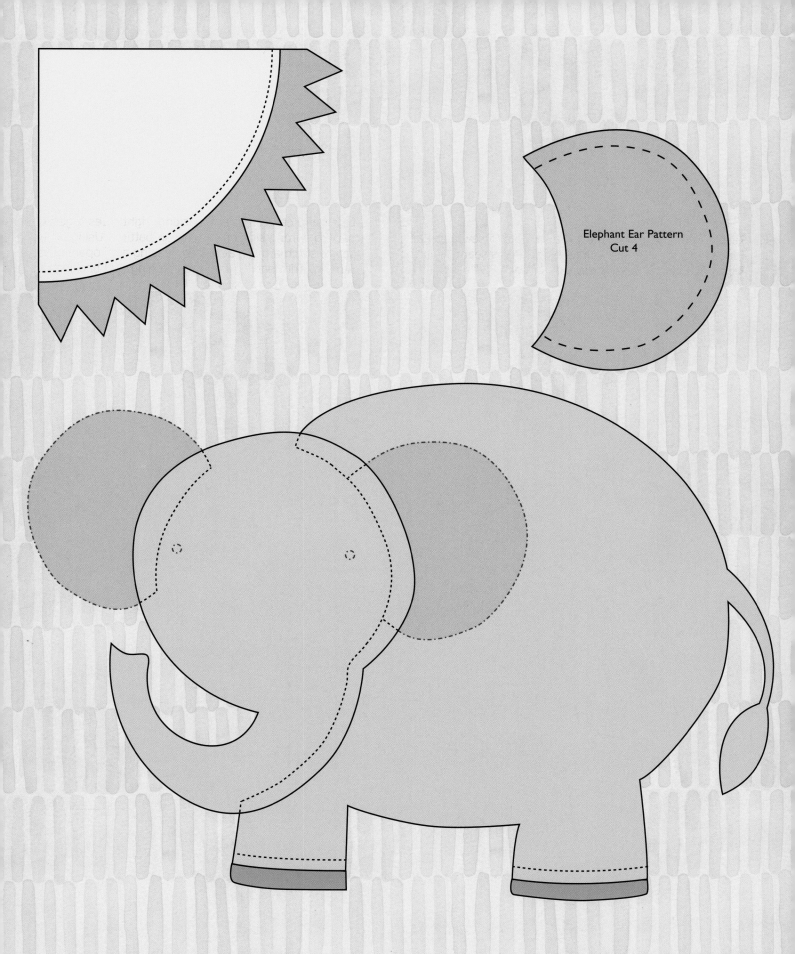

Elephant Ear Pattern
Cut 4

Lion Pillow

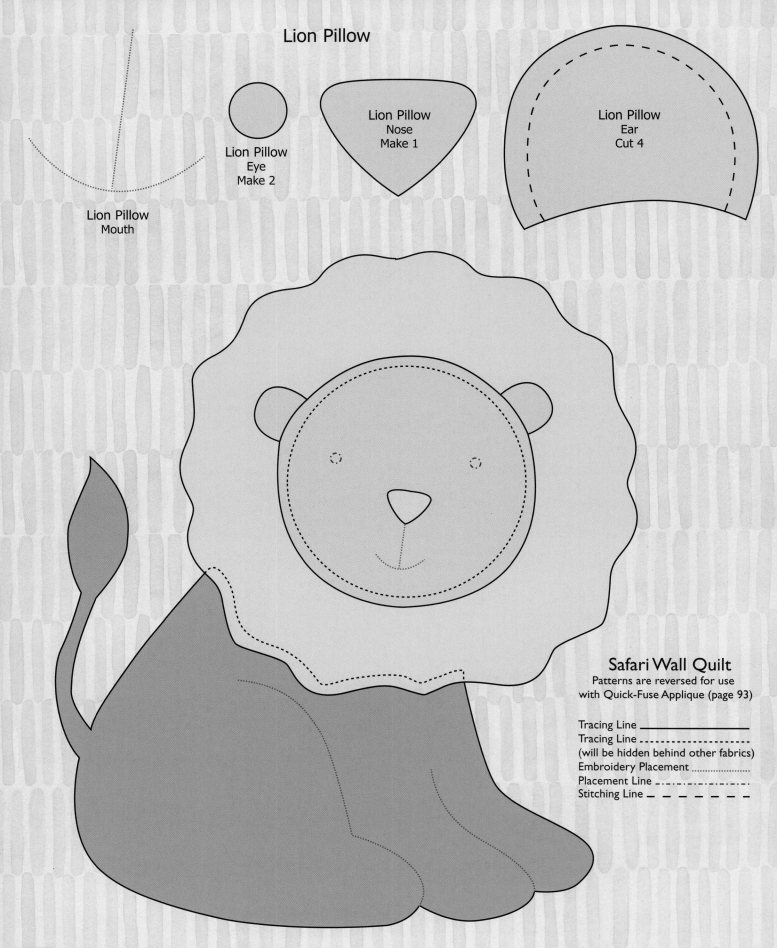

Lion Pillow
Eye
Make 2

Lion Pillow
Nose
Make 1

Lion Pillow
Ear
Cut 4

Lion Pillow
Mouth

Safari Wall Quilt
Patterns are reversed for use with Quick-Fuse Applique (page 93)

Tracing Line _____
Tracing Line - - - - - - - - - - - - - -
(will be hidden behind other fabrics)
Embroidery Placement ....
Placement Line - · - · - · - · - · - ·
Stitching Line — — — — — —

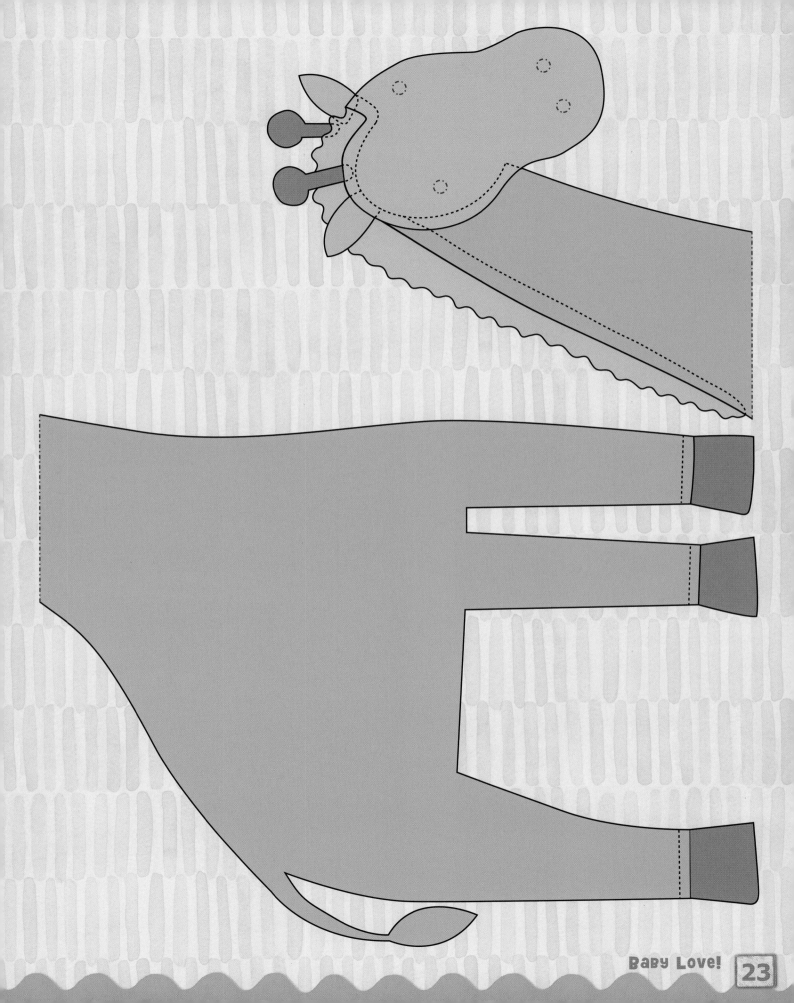

SILLY SAFARI
CRIB QUILT

Silly Safari Crib Quilt Finished Size: 42" x 52"	FIRST CUT	
	Number of Strips or Pieces	Dimensions
Fabric A Rail Fence ⅓ yard each of five fabrics	4*	2½" x 42" *cut for each fabric
Fabric B Rail Fence ⅓ yard each of five fabrics	4*	2½" x 42" *cut for each fabric
Binding ⅔ yard	6	3½" x 42"
Backing - 2⅝ yards Batting - 47" x 57" Rickrack - 5 yards		

Fabric Requirements and Cutting Instructions

Read all instructions before beginning and use ¼"-wide seam allowances throughout. Read Cutting Strips and Pieces on page 92 prior to cutting fabric.

Getting Started

It's a jungle in here! Create a joyful jungle for a little one with this easy quilt that perfectly complements the wall quilt. Rail Fence Blocks measure 10½" square (unfinished). Refer to Accurate Seam Allowance on page 92. Whenever possible use the Assembly Line Method on page 92. Press seams in the direction of arrows.

1. Sew together lengthwise five 2½" x 42" assorted Fabric A strips. Press. Make four. Cut strip sets into ten 10½"-wide segments as shown.

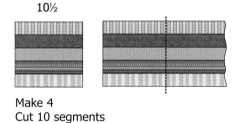

10½

Make 4
Cut 10 segments

2. Sew together lengthwise five 2½" x 42" assorted Fabric B strips. Press. Make four. Cut strip sets into ten 10½"-wide segments as shown.

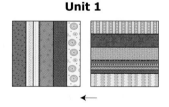

10½

Make 4
Cut 10 segments

3. Sew one block from step 1 and one block from step 2 together as shown. Press. Make six, and label Unit 1.

Unit 1

Make 6

4. Sew one block from step 2 and one block from step 1 together as shown. Press. Make four, and label Unit 2.

Unit 2

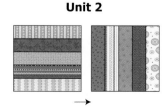

Make 4

5. Refer to layout on page 26 for Row 1 block orientation. Arrange and sew together two of Unit 1. Press seams in one direction. Make three.

6. Refer to layout on page 26 for Row 2 block orientation. Arrange and sew together two of Unit 2. Press seams in opposite direction from previous sewn rows. Make two.

7. Referring to layout on page 26, arrange and sew rows from step 5 and 6 together. Press.

Layering and Finishing

1. Cut backing crosswise into two equal pieces. Sew pieces together lengthwise to make one 47" x 80" (approximate) backing piece. Press and trim to 47" x 57".

2. Referring to Layering the Quilt on page 94, arrange and baste backing, batting, and top together. Hand or machine quilt as desired.

3. Refer to Binding the Quilt on page 94. Sew 3½" x 42" binding strips end-to-end to make one continuous 3½"-wide binding strip. Bind quilt to finish. Note: This binding is wider than our normal width. Trim batting and backing to ¾" beyond raw edge of quilt. Binding finishes 1"-wide.

4. Refer to photo to sew rickrack to quilt placing it at quilt top outside edges next to binding.

SILLY SAFARI CRIB QUILT
Finished Size: 42" x 52"

Oversized rail fence blocks make this quilt fast and easy, but the colors really make it fun. Rickrack trim adds the final bit of pizzazz to this cute quilt.

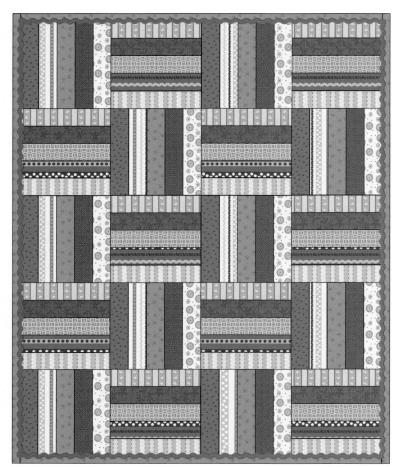

SILLY SAFARI CRIB QUILT Finished Size: 42" x 52"

Follow block construction on page 24

MAKE IT TWIN SIZE

Follow block construction on page 24 to make forty-eight blocks, twenty-four of each from step 1 and 2. Make twelve each of Unit 1 and 2. Assemble eight rows of three units each, alternating unit placement from row to row.

Silly Safari Twin Bed Quilt Finished Size: 61" x 81" Make 24 of each Block	FIRST CUT	
	Number of Strips or Pieces	Dimensions
Fabric A Rail Fence ⅔ yard each of five fabrics	8*	2½" x 42" *cut for each fabric
Fabric B Rail Fence ⅔ yard each of five fabrics	8*	2½" x 42" *cut for each fabric
Binding 1 yard	8	3½" x 42"
Backing - 5 yards Batting - 68" x 88" Rickrack - 8 yards		

Silly Safari WHEELIES

SUPPLIES

Unfinished Wood Animals with Wheels

Acrylic Craft Paints — Americana® Bahama Blue, Raw Sienna, Lt. Avocado, Jack-o'-lantern Orange; Delta Ceramcoat® Spice Brown, Light Foliage Green, Poppy Orange, Bamboo, Forest Green; black, white

Assorted Paintbrushes, Circles Template, Sandpaper, Gesso, Gloss Varnish, Tack Cloth, Orange Rickrack, Clear Tacky Glue

1. Refer to General Painting Directions on page 95. Apply Gesso to all surfaces and allow to dry. Lightly sand animals to get a smooth surface. Remove residue with tack cloth.

2. Basecoat elephant with Raw Sienna for body, Jack-o'-lantern Orange for ear, and Bahama Blue for wheels.

3. Using circles template and pencil, draw ⅜" circles randomly on elephant body. Paint dots and outline ear with Spice Brown Paint. When dry, lightly sand dots to soften edges.

4. Using Raw Sienna, dry brush texture on ears. When dry, use fine brush and Poppy Orange to paint a cross-hatch line pattern on ear.

5. Paint center of wheel with Bamboo paint and add an orange dot in the center.

6. Use end of small paintbrush and black paint to make a dot eye for elephant. Add a tiny spot of white paint for highlight.

7. Basecoat giraffe with Forest Green for body and Bamboo for wheels. Using photo as a guide, use circle template and pencil to draw circles of various sizes onto giraffe body. Using Lt. Avocado and Light Foliage Green paint, paint circles.

8. Paint inside of wheels Bahama Blue and add a dot of Jack-o'-lantern orange in the center. Repeat procedure in step 6 to make an eye for giraffe. When animals are thoroughly dry apply several coats of gloss varnish. Glue orange rickrack to giraffe neck and head to create a mane.

Lion
PILLOW

Baby will roar with delight when this smiling lion greets him each night. A fleece mane and wiggly ears add fun dimension to this silly pillow that will carry the safari theme to any part of the nursery.

Lion Pillow Finished Size: 16" circle	FIRST CUT	
	Number of Strips or Pieces	Dimensions
Fabric A Background ⅝ yard	2	17½" squares
Fabric B Lion Mane - Fleece ¼ yard	1	3½" x 45"
Fabric C Lion Face ⅓ yard		
Appliqués - Assorted Scraps Iron-on interfacing - ½ yard Lightweight Fusible Web - ⅓ yard Polyester fiberfill Yard Stick and Compass Points		

Making the Pillow

1. Referring to manufacturer's instructions, fuse iron-on interfacing to wrong side of one 17½" Fabric A square.

2. Using a yardstick and compass points draw a 16½" circle and 9¼" circle on pattern paper. Cut on traced lines. Cut two 16½" circles from 17½" Fabric A squares.

3. Trace (on the right side) a 9¼" circle centering it on 16½" Fabric A circle with interfacing.

4. Clip 3½" x 45" Fabric B strip every ¼" to ½", 3" into fleece along long side to make fringed mane. Leave ½" on opposite side free of clippings. Pin uncut edge of fleece along 9¼" traced circle as shown, overlapping mane ends slightly. Baste in place.

5. Using a yardstick and compass points, draw a 9¾" circle on paper side of lightweight-fusible web. Referring to manufacturer's instructions fuse circle to wrong side of Fabric C piece. Cut on drawn line.

6. Use patterns on page 22 to trace lion nose and two eyes on paper side of fusible web. Use appropriate fabrics to prepare all appliqués for fusing.

7. Refer to photo to position and fuse appliqués to 9¾" Fabric C circle. Using removable fabric marker, transfer lion mouth embroidery lines (page 22) to circle unit.

8. Trace lion ear (page 22) on pattern paper or template plastic. Cut on drawn line. Trace four ears on wrong side of fabric piece, two regular and two reversed. Cut on drawn line. Place two ears, one of each variation, right sides together. Stitch using ¼"-wide seam around outside curve only, leaving inside curve free of stitching for turning. Clip curve, turn right side out, and press. Take a small tuck in center of raw edge and baste in place. Repeat for other ear.

9. Refer to photo to position ears ¼" under outer edge of lion face and fuse in place covering mane's inside edge. Finish appliqué edges with machine satin stitch or other decorative stitching as desired. Using a machine satin stitch, stitch mouth on drawn lines. Optional: Refer to embroidery guide on page 23 and using a stem stitch and three strands of embroidery floss, stitch mouth lines.

Finishing the Pillow

1. Layer lion circle unit with 16½" Fabric A circle right sides together. Using a ¼"-wide seam allowance, stitch, leaving a 6" opening for turning. Clip curves and turn right side out. Press.

2. Stuff pillow with fiberfill to desired fullness. Hand stitch opening closed.

Baby Blooms Crib Quilt

Baby Blooms Crib Quilt Finished Size: 41" x 60"	FIRST CUT		SECOND CUT	
	Number of Strips or Pieces	Dimensions	Number of Pieces	Dimensions
Fabric A Background ⅞ yard	2 1	11½" x 42" 5" x 42"	2 1	11½" x 38½" 5" x 38½"
Fabric B First Accent Border ¼ yard	2	3½" x 42"	2	3½" x 38½"
Fabric C Second Accent Border ½ yard	2	7" x 42"	2	7" x 38½"
Fabric D Third Accent Border ⅜ yard	2 5	2" x 42" 1½" x 42"	2 2	2" x 38½" 1½" x 38½"
Fabric E Fourth Accent Border ¼ yard	2	2½" x 42"	2	2½" x 38½"
Binding ⅝ yard	6	2¾" x 42"		

Backing - 2⅝ yards
Batting - 47" x 66"
Appliqué Flowers & Leaves - Assorted Scraps
Appliqué Stem Trims - 1 yard each of three trims
Quilt Trims - 2½ yards Rickrack trim
2½ yards ¼"-wide trim
1⅛ yard each of three assorted trims
Lightweight Fusible Web - ¾ yard

Fabric Requirements and Cutting Instructions

Read all instructions before beginning and use ¼"-wide seam allowances throughout. Read Cutting Strips and Pieces on page 92 prior to cutting fabric.

Getting Started

Pink and purple flowers dance across this quilt while an accent of assorted trims adds dimension. Refer to Accurate Seam Allowance on page 92. Whenever possible use the Assembly Line Method on page 92. Press seams in the direction of arrows.

Making the Quilt

Refer to appliqué instructions on page 93. Our instructions are for Quick-Fuse Appliqué, but if you prefer hand appliqué, add ¼"-wide seam allowances.

1. Refer to photo on page 29 to arrange and sew together two 3½" x 38½" Fabric B strips, two 7" x 38½" Fabric C strips, two 2" x 38½" Fabric D strips, two 11½" x 38½" Fabric A strips, two 1½" x 38½" Fabric D strips, two 2½" x 38½" Fabric E strips, and one 5" x 38½" Fabric A strip. Press seams toward larger fabric pieces.

2. Use patterns on pages 30-31 to trace four each of Flower #2 and #3, two of Flower #1, four of Leaf #1, ten of Leaf #2, four of Leaf #3, and four of leaf #3 reversed, on paper side of fusible web. Use appropriate fabrics to prepare all appliqués for fusing.

3. Refer to photo on page 29 to position flowers on quilt. Cut trim for stems, determine position and un-stitch quilt seam to insert bottom end of trim. Pin trim in place, stitch trim to quilt and re-stitch quilt seam. Repeat for bottom flower panel. Following manufacturer's instructions, fuse flowers and leaves to quilt top.

4. Finish appliqué edges with machine satin stitch or other decorative stitching as desired.

5. Referring to photo on page 29, position trims on quilt and stitch in place. Note: We used rickrack trim on both top and bottom section of quilt aligning trim next to Fabric B and C seam lines, ¼"-wide trim aligned next to Fabric A and E seams, and the remaining three trims are arranged in the center of quilt.

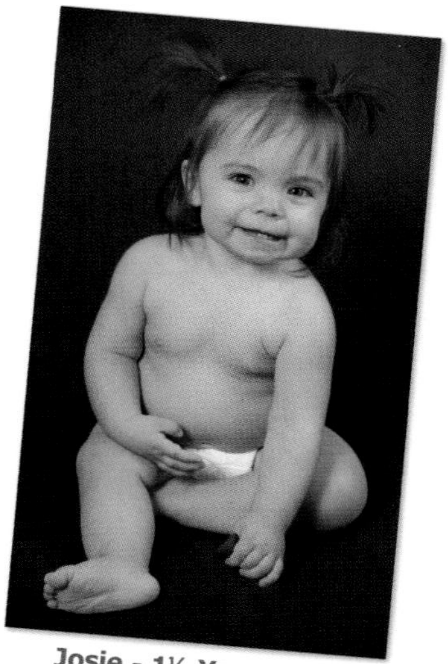

Josie - 1½ Years Old

6. Sew 1½" Fabric D strips end-to-end to make one continuous 1½"-wide Fabric D strip. Measure quilt from top to bottom and cut two strips to this measurement. Sew to sides of quilt. Press.

Layering and Finishing

1. Cut backing crosswise into two equal pieces. Sew pieces together lengthwise to make one 47" x 80" (approximate) backing piece. Press and trim to 47" x 66".

2. Referring to Layering the Quilt on page 94, arrange and baste backing, batting, and top together. Hand or machine quilt as desired.

3. Refer to Binding the Quilt on page 94. Sew 2¾" x 42" binding strips end-to-end to make one continuous 2¾"-wide binding strip. Bind quilt to finish.

Baby blooms and so does her crib quilt! Pretty pink and purple flowers reach for the sun in this easy strip-pieced quilt. Ribbon trim highlights the center section and bold rickrack adds dimension and added design. Have some fun selecting fabrics and trims for this fresh and flowery quilt!

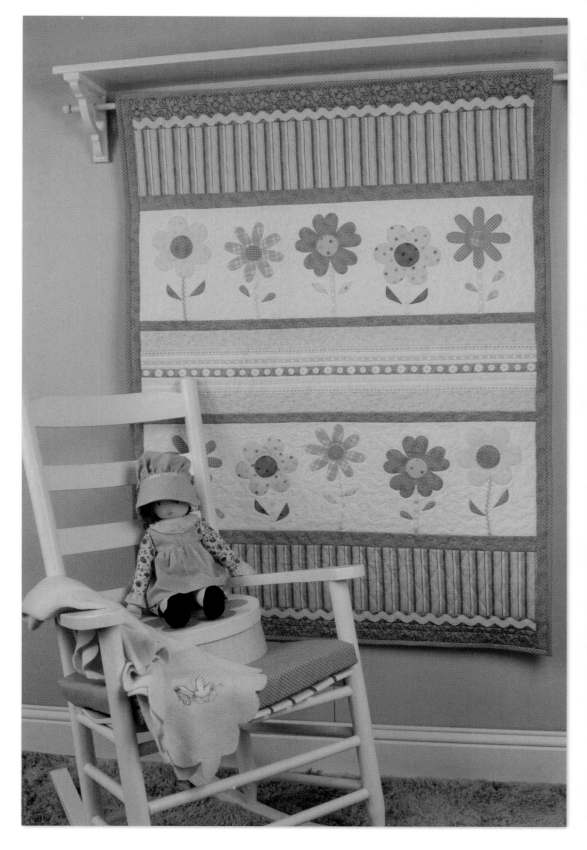

BABY BLOOMS CRIB QUILT
Finished Size: 41" x 60"

Flower #1
Make 2

Leaf #1
Make 4

Baby Blooms Crib Quilt

Tracing Line ─────────

Permission is granted by Debbie Mumm Inc.
to copy page 30-31 to successfully complete project.

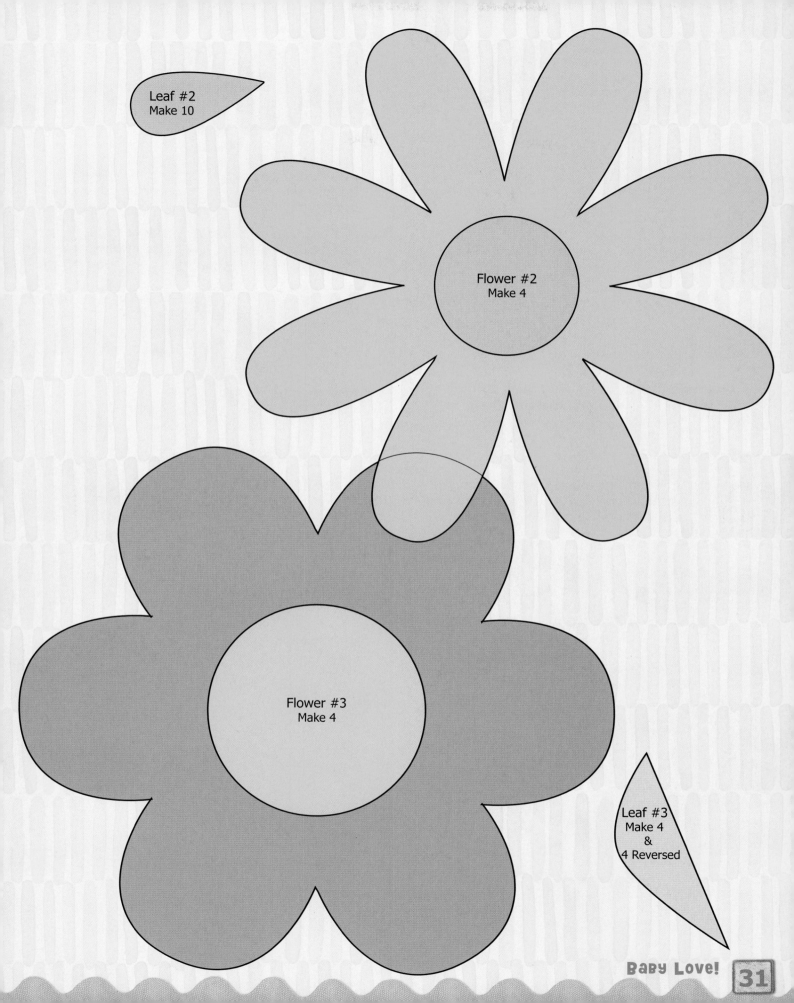

Leaf #2
Make 10

Flower #2
Make 4

Flower #3
Make 4

Leaf #3
Make 4
&
4 Reversed

Baby Love!

BABY BLOOMS WINDOW VALANCE

The bright morning sun will peek through
the posies when you match a fresh
blooming valance to the crib quilt.

Making the Valance

1. Refer to photo to arrange and sew together one 5½" x 38½" Fabric C strip, one 2" x 38½" Fabric B strip, one 11½" x 38½" Fabric A strip and one 1¾" x 38½" Fabric B strip. Press.

2. Refer to Quick-Fuse Applique on page 93. Use patterns on pages 30-31 and fabric scraps to prepare flower appliqués. Position flowers on Fabric A strip. Determine position for trim stems, pin in place, trim, and stitch to quilt. Fuse flowers in place and finish edges as desired.

3. Sew unit between two 1½" x 19¼" Fabric B. Strips. Press.

4. Place backing and valance right sides together. Using ¼"-wide seam, sew top and bottom edges. Turn right side out and press, making sure that ¼"-wide bottom border turns evenly to back side.

5. Turn right sides together bottom is folded along pressing line and hem seam is ¼" away from fold. Using ¼"-wide seam, sew one side edge, starting 2" from top edge. [Adjust this measurement for larger rod pocket.] Repeat for other side but leave a 5" opening for turning. Clip corners, turn right side out, and press.

6. Measure rod pocket distance from top edge and mark with removable fabric marker, and stitch through all thicknesses to make pocket.

Kate - 7 Months Old

Baby Blooms Valance Finished Size: 40" x 18½"	FIRST CUT	
	Number of Pieces	Dimensions
Fabric A Background	1	11½" x 38½"
Fabric B First Accent Border	1	2" x 38½"
	1	1¾" x 38½"
	2	1½" x 19¼"
Fabric C Second Accent Border	1	5½" x 38½"
Backing - 18¾" x 40½" Appliqués - Assorted scraps Lightweight Fusible Web - ½ yard Stems - Various ribbons and rickrack trims		

Blooming
HAT BOXES

Making the Decorative Hat Boxes

We chose to use craft paints on the second and bottom boxes and a combination of scrapbook paper and paint on the top and third box. If desired, wallpaper can be used in place of scrapbook paper.

Refer to General Painting Directions on page 95. Prime boxes and lids with Gesso and allow to dry. Lightly sand boxes and lids for a smooth painting surface and remove residue with tack cloth.

Box 1 (Smallest/Top Box): Paint lid with Baby Pink. Two or more coats may be needed for good coverage. Measure sides of box and cut selected scrapbook paper to that measurement. Use craft glue to glue paper to the sides of hat box. If several pieces of paper are needed to cover, be sure to match patterns on paper before cutting. If desired, enlarge Flower #3 pattern on page 31 to a size to fit the lid and use paper or fabric to make a flower and center. Glue to lid. Apply matte vanish to painted surfaces.

Box 2: Paint lid and box warm white. To create plaid, use ruler and pencil to draw horizontal stripes on sides of hat box. Stripes should be 1" wide with ½" between stripes. Use Touch O Pink paint to paint each 1"-wide stripe. Allow to dry thoroughly. Repeat stripe pattern vertically, again painting each 1"-wide stripe Touch O Pink. When thoroughly dry, use Baby Pink to darken squares where stripes overlap. Sand hat box to soften edges and "age" the new paint. Remove sanding residue with a tack cloth. Using a fine brush and Pansy paint diluted with water, hand paint purple lines as shown in photo. When completely dry, apply matte varnish to painted surfaces. Glue rickrack trim to lid edge.

Box 3: Paint lid Warm White and glue on ribbon trim when dry. Use scrapbook paper to cover sides of hat box following procedure for Box 1.

Box 4: Paint lid with Bubble Gum. When dry, use ruler and pencil to draw 1" stripes around edge of lid. Paint every other stripe with Touch O Pink. If desired, use 1" circle template to draw dots on top of lid. Paint with Touch O Pink. Paint sides of hat box with Warm White. Use 2" circle template to draw large dots on sides of box. Use Touch O Pink to paint dots. Allow to dry thoroughly before varnishing.

Create storage for baby's little treasures and an eye-catching decoration with these handsome hat boxes. Select from a variety of techniques or mix and match as we did by using both paints and papers to decorate the hat boxes.

Set of Four Nesting Wood or Papier Mâché Hat Boxes

Sandpaper and Tack Cloth

Gesso

Acrylic Craft Paints — FolkArt® Warm White and Baby Pink; Delta Ceramcoat® Bubble Gum, Touch O Pink, and Pansy

Matte Varnish

Assorted Paintbrushes

Assorted Decorative Trims

Assorted Scrapbook Papers

Elmer's Craft Bond™ Paper Craft Glue Gel

Scissors, Ruler, Pencil, Paper Cutter, 1" and 2" Circle Templates (page 95)

BABY BLOOMS
GROWTH CHART

SUPPLIES

10" x 36" MDF (Medium-Density Fiberboard)

Gesso

Acrylic Craft Paints — FolkArt® Warm White; Delta Ceramcoat® Touch O Pink

Assorted Paintbrushes

Sandpaper and Tack Cloth

Assorted Fabric Scraps for Flowers, Centers, and Leaves

Assorted Trims for Stems and Flower Centers

Assorted Buttons

Heavyweight Fusible Web

Clear Fabric Glue

Micron 005 Pigma Pen with Archival Ink (Available at Art and Quilt Stores)

Ruler, Pencil, 2" Circle Template (page 95)

Ava - 2 Months Old

Keep track as Baby blooms and grows with this decorative and darling growth chart. Subtle painted stripes form a backdrop for appliquéd flowers that reach for the sky. Inch marks along one side allow you to mark the growth progress of your little one with a permanent notation.

Making the Growth Chart

1. Refer to General Painting Directions on page 95. Apply Gesso to MDF Board and allow to dry. Lightly sand until smooth and remove residue with tack cloth.

2. Apply Warm White paint to prepared board. Two or more coats of paint may be needed for good coverage. Allow paint to dry thoroughly after each coat.

3. Referring to photo, use pencil and ruler to mark 1" stripes on lower portion of board. Using 2" circle template mark circles as desired on top half of board. Place some partial circles at sides and along diagonal line.

4. Paint every other stripe with Touch O Pink. Paint marked circles with Touch O Pink. Two or more coats of paint may be necessary for good coverage. Allow to dry overnight.

5. Lightly sand painted area to soften lines and add subtle shading. Remove sanding residue with tack cloth.

6. Refer to Quick Fuse Applique on Page 93. Using Flower #1 and Flower #2 patterns on pages 30 and 31, fabric scraps, and heavyweight fusible web, prepare two flowers. Prepare an assortment of leaves in same manner.

7. For Flower #3, we enlarged pattern on page 31 to 115% for dimensional flower and reduced it 80% for smallest flower. If a copier isn't available, sketch larger and smaller versions of the pattern and use your prepared pattern.

8. After reducing Flower #3 pattern, prepare flower using Quick Fuse Appliqué directions on page 93.

9. To make dimensional flower, place two matching pieces of fabric right sides together and use enlarged pattern to cut two flower shapes. Using ¼" seams, sew around edges of flower, clipping fabric to the seams at petal points. Cut a slit in the back, and turn flower right side out.

10. Referring to photo, determine placement of flowers and decorative trim stems. Use glue to adhere trim stems to painted board. If available, use a small appliqué iron to adhere quick-fuse flowers to board. If a mini-iron isn't available, use glue to adhere appliqués. Using a full size iron may damage the painted surface.

11. A ribbon ruffle is the center of the dimensional flower. Start with a single loop, and continue adding loops (making sure print side is up), fanning loops into a circle as shown in bottom photo. Use a straight pin to hold loops in place temporarily. Place ruffle on dimensional flower then sew a button in the center of the ribbon ruffle, making sure to sew through all layers of ribbon and through the center of the dimensional flower. Glue completed dimensional flower in place.

12. Refer to photo to add centers to remaining flowers. Refer to step 6 to prepare leaves, determine placement, then glue or use mini-iron to adhere.

13. Using ruler and pencil, draw inch marks on right side of Growth Chart. Use pigma pen and small ruler to mark straight, ½"-wide, inch marks over the pencil mark.

14. Mount Growth Chart on wall, exactly 2' from floor. Use colored pigma pen to mark each measurement date and height.

GIRLY GIRLS

Tender girls love butterflies and blooms, hearts, sparkles, and pink rooms.

Lena - 3 Years Old

A little princess deserves a castle filled with softness and sweet symbols of love and tenderness. Create her perfect palace - full of fluttering butterflies or hearts and flowers - where she can snuggle under the warmth and comfort of your love.

FLUTTERBY TWIN BED QUILT

Fabric Requirements and Cutting Instructions

Read all instructions before beginning and use ¼"-wide seam allowances throughout. Read Cutting Strips and Pieces on page 92 prior to cutting fabric.

Flutterby Twin Bed Quilt Finished Size: 64" x 79"	FIRST CUT	
	Number of Strips or Pieces	Dimensions
Fabric A Background ½ yard each of six fabrics	9*	12½" squares *Total needed - cut from assorted fabrics
Fabric B Large Nine-Patch ⅓ yard each of nine fabrics	2**	4½" x 42" **cut for each fabric
Fabric C Small Nine-Patch Dark ½ yard	8	1½" x 42"
Fabric D Small Nine-Patch Light ⅜ yard	7	1½" x 42"
Fabric E Lattice Dark 1⅝ yards	34	1½" x 42"
Fabric F Lattice Light ⅞ yard	17	1½" x 42"
Binding ¾ yard	8	2¾" x 42"

Butterfly Appliqués - Assorted Scraps
Backing - 4⅞ yards
Batting - 72" x 87"
Lightweight Fusible Web - 1 yard
Embroidery Floss

Getting Started

Butterflies flutter in a field of nine-patch blocks in this quilt. Blocks measure 12½" square (unfinished). Refer to Accurate Seam Allowance on page 92. Whenever possible use the Assembly Line Method on page 92. Press seams in the direction of arrows.

Making the Nine-Patch Blocks

1. Sew three 4½" x 42" Fabric B strips together lengthwise to make a strip set. Press seams toward center. Make six, two of each combination. Cut strip sets into thirty-three 4½"-wide segments, eleven of each combination as shown. Note: Repress eleven segments away from center.

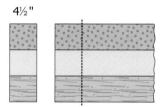

4½"

Make 6
(2 of each combination)
Cut 33 segments
(11 of each combination)

2. Arrange and sew three strip sets from step 1, one of each combination, together as shown. Press. Make eleven large Nine-Patch blocks. Blocks measure 12½" square.

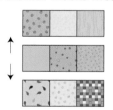

Make 11
Block measures 12½" square

3. Sew lengthwise one 1½" x 42" Fabric D strip between two 1½" x 42" Fabric C strips to make a strip set. Press seams toward Fabric C. Make three. Cut strip set into sixty 1½"-wide segments as shown.

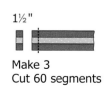

1½"

Make 3
Cut 60 segments

4. Sew lengthwise one 1½" x 42" Fabric C strip between two 1½" x 42" Fabric D strips to make a strip set. Press seams toward Fabric C. Make two. Cut strip set into thirty 1½"-wide segments.

1½"

Make 2
Cut 30 segments

5. Sew one segment from step 4 between two segments from step 3 as shown. Press. Make thirty small Nine-Patch units. Units measure 3½" square.

Make 30

Making the Butterfly Blocks

Refer to appliqué instructions on page 93. Our instructions are for Quick-Fuse Appliqué, but if you prefer hand appliqué, reverse templates and add ¼"-wide seam allowances.

1. Use pattern on page 41 to trace six butterflies on paper side of fusible web. Note: For each butterfly trace one regular and one reversed pattern for each wing section. Use appropriate fabrics to prepare all appliqués for fusing.

2. Refer to layout on page 40 and photo to position and fuse butterflies to six 12½" Fabric A squares. Finish appliqué edges with machine satin stitch or other decorative stitching as desired. Embroider antennae by hand or machine.

FLUTTERBY TWIN BED QUILT
Finished Size: 64" x 79"

Beautiful butterflies flutter across a field of nine-patch blocks softened by squares of lustrous minky on this heartwarming quilt. Your little one will love the sweet colors, patterns, and feel of this quilt which is sure to become one of her favorite childhood memories.

FLUTTERBY TWIN BED QUILT Finished Size: 64" x 79"

Assembly

1. Sew lengthwise one 1½" x 42" Fabric F strip between two 1½" x 42" Fabric E strips to make a strip set. Press toward Fabric F. Make seventeen. Cut strip set into forty-nine 12½"-wide lattice segments as shown.

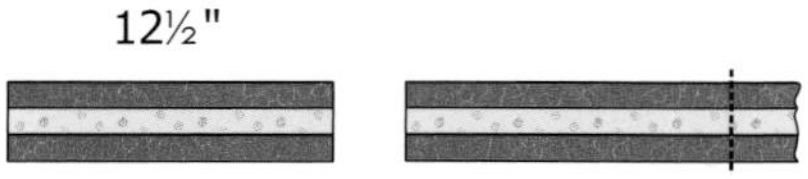

Make 17
Cut 49 segments

2. Refer to photo on page 39 and layout to arrange and sew together five small Nine-Patch units and four units from step 1. Press seams toward lattice. Make six rows.
3. Refer to photo on page 39 and layout to arrange and sew together five units from step 1, one Butterfly block, and three Nine-Patch Blocks. Press seams toward lattice. Make two.
4. Refer to photo on page 39 and layout to arrange and sew together five units from step 1, two Butterfly blocks, one 12½" Fabric A square, and one Nine-Patch Block. Press seams toward lattice.
5. Refer to photo on page 39 and layout to arrange and sew together five units from step 1, one Butterfly block, one 12½" Fabric A square, and two Nine-Patch Blocks. Press toward strip set. Make two.
6. Refer to photo on page 39 and layout to arrange and sew together rows from steps 1-5. Press.

Layering and Finishing

1. Cut backing crosswise into two equal pieces. Sew pieces together lengthwise to make one 80" x 87" (approximate) backing piece. Press.
2. Referring to Layering the Quilt on page 94, arrange and baste backing, batting, and top together. Hand or machine quilt as desired.
3. Sew 2¾" x 42" binding strips end-to-end to make one continuous 2¾"-wide binding strip. Refer to Binding the Quilt on page 94 and bind quilt to finish.

MAKE IT CRIB SIZE

Flutterby Crib Quilt Finished Size: 34" x 49" Refer to Flutterby instructions (pages 38-41) to make four Large Nine-Patch Blocks, two Butterfly Blocks, twelve Nine-Patch units and seventeen Lattice segments.	FIRST CUT	
	Number of Strips or Pieces	Dimensions
Fabric A Background ⅜ yard each of two fabrics	1*	12½" squares *cut for each fabric
Fabric B Large Nine-Patch ⅙ yard each of nine fabrics	1*	4½" x 42" *cut for each fabric (Make strip set and cut four segments of each.)
Fabric C Small Nine-Patch Dark ⅙ yard	3	1½" x 42"
Fabric D Small Nine-Patch Light ⅙ yard	3	1½" x 42"
Fabric E Lattice Dark ⅝ yard	12	1½" x 42"
Fabric F Lattice Light ⅓ yard	6	1½" x 42"
Binding ½ yard	5	2¾" x 42"
Butterfly Appliqués - Assorted Scraps Backing - 1⅝ yards Batting - 40" x 55" Lightweight Fusible Web - ½ yard Embroidery Floss		

Flutterby Quilt

Tracing Line ————————
Tracing Line - - - - - - - - - - - -
(will be hidden behind other fabrics)
Embroidery Placement ....
Placement Line - · - · - · - · - · -

Wings
Make 1 and
1 Reversed
for each
Butterfly

FLUTTERBY PILLOW SHAM

Flutterby Pillow Sham Finished Size: 20" x 26"	FIRST CUT	
	Number of Strips or Pieces	Dimensions
Fabric A Background ¾ yard	1 6	14½" x 20½" 1½" x 42"
Fabric B Accent Border ¼ yard	3	1½" x 42"
Fabric C Mock Piping ⅙ yard	2 2	1½" x 20½" 1½" x 14½"
Backing ⅔ yard	1 1	20½" square 20½" x 11½"

Appliqués - Assorted Scraps
Batting - 24" x 30"
Lining - ⅔ yard
Lightweight Fusible Web - ¼ yard
Embroidery Floss
Beads (Optional)
Pillow Form Fabric (Optional) - ½ yard
    Two 14½" x 20½"
Polyester Fiberfill (Optional)

Getting Started

This "pretty-in-pink" pillow is sure to be a hit for the little girl in your life. Use it to dress-up her bed or accent her favorite chair. Use this pattern to make a pillow sham for a standard bed pillow or stitch-in-the-ditch to create a smaller pillow with flange. Read all instructions before beginning and use ¼"-wide seam allowances throughout.

Adding the Appliqués

Refer to appliqué instructions on page 93. Our instructions are for Quick-Fuse Appliqué, but if you prefer hand appliqué, add ¼"-wide seam allowances.

1. Use pattern on page 41 to trace butterfly on paper side of fusible web. Note: Trace one regular and one reversed pattern for each wing section. Use appropriate fabrics to prepare all appliqués for fusing.

2. Refer to photo to position and fuse appliqués to 14½" x 20½" Fabric A piece. Finish appliqué edges with machine satin stitch or other decorative stitching as desired. Embroider antennae by hand or machine. Optional: Add beads for eyes and antennae ends.

Making the Pillow

1. Fold 1½" x 20½" and 14½" Fabric C strips in half lengthwise wrong sides together. Press.

2. Matching raw edges, layer folded strips from step 1 on appliqué unit as shown. Baste in place.

3. Sew one 1½" x 42" Fabric B strip between two 1½" x 42" Fabric A strips as shown. Press. Make three. Cut side unit in half crosswise.

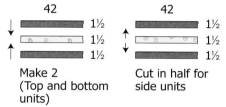

Make 2 (Top and bottom units)

Cut in half for side units

4. Refer to Mitered Borders on page 94. Sew top, bottom and side units from step 3 to unit from step 2 mitering corners. Press seams away from center.

5. Refer to Finishing Pillows on page 95, step 1, to prepare pillow top for quilting. Quilt as desired.

6. Use one 20½" square and one 20½" x 11½" backing pieces and refer to Finishing Pillows, page 95, steps 2-4, to sew backing.

7. Insert standard pillow for pillow sham or to create a pillow with flange, stitch-in-the-ditch between appliqué center and border unit. Refer to Pillow Forms page 95 to make a 14" x 20" pillow form.

Name in
FRAMES

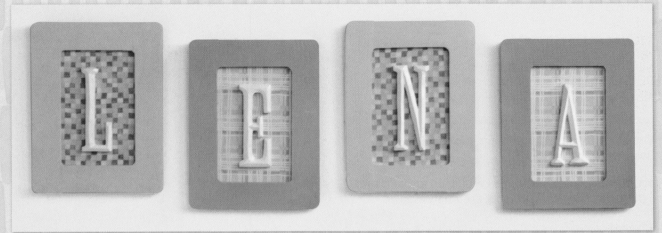

Almost as sweet and pretty as she is...every little girl will love to see her name in frames and mounted on her wall. The perfect artwork for a princess's palace, this project is fast and fun. Change paint colors to match her room or use our paint color choices.

Making the Project

1. Refer to General Painting Directions on page 95. Lightly sand letters and frames and remove residue with a damp cloth.

2. Paint letters with Wicker White. Two or more coats of paint may be needed for good coverage. Allow paint to dry thoroughly after each coat.

3. Paint two frames Baby Pink, applying two or more coats as needed. Paint two frames with a mixture of 2 parts Eucalyptus and 2 parts Hauser Green Light (or mixed as desired). Two or more coats of paint may be needed for good coverage.

4. Frames usually come with a cardboard insert. Trace the size of this insert onto scrapbook paper and cut out. Use paper craft glue to glue scrapbook paper to cardboard insert and fasten into frame.

5. Using tacky glue, apply glue to each letter and center in frame. Allow to dry thoroughly before hanging on wall.

4"-Tall Wood Letters to Spell Name

Wood Frame for Each Letter
Ours are 6¼" x 8¼" with an opening 4" x 6"

Scrapbook Paper*

Acrylic Craft Paint — FolkArt® Baby Pink, Wicker White, and Hauser Green Light; Delta Ceramcoat® Eucalyptus

Matte Varnish

Assorted Paint Brushes

Tacky Glue

Sandpaper

*Debbie Mumm® scrapbook products are available at Jo-Ann Fabric and Craft Stores.

BUTTERFLY BLING

Decked with bright baubles, this beautiful butterfly will wing its way into a little girl's heart! Paint, scrapbook paper, beads, and bling dress up a simple wood butterfly form with princess-worthy panache.

Making the Butterfly

1. Refer to General Painting Directions on page 95. If needed, sand butterfly cut-out and remove residue with damp cloth.

2. Apply Gesso to butterfly and allow to dry. Lightly sand butterfly again for a smooth painting surface. Remove residue with damp cloth.

3. Mix 1 part Royal Fuchsia to 3 parts Bubble Gum paint and apply to butterfly. Two or more coats of paint may be needed for good coverage. Allow paint to dry thoroughly after each coat.

4. Apply Royal Fuchsia paint to butterfly edges. Allow to dry. Paint antennae with Festive Green.

5. To make a pattern for the wings, trace butterfly shape onto piece of scrap paper. Using a pencil, place a series of dots about 1" from wing edges (on one side) and about ½" from "body." Using dots as a guide, draw a large and small egg-shaped form to be pattern for wing embellishments.

6. Using pattern and card stock, cut two large upper wing egg shapes and two lower wing smaller egg shapes. Place on wood butterfly to check for fit and make any alterations desired.

7. Using pattern and scrapbook paper, trace pattern. Cut ½" inside pattern lines to make two smaller upper and lower wing pieces.

8. Glue scrapbook paper pieces to cardstock wing pieces. Referring to photo, use foam mounting tape to attach wings to painted butterfly.

9. Use bead glue to adhere large green beads for butterfly body. Use an acrylic stone flower as a head and glue round acrylic stone to center of flower and to ends of antennae.

10. String assorted green, lavender, and pink beads on a heavy wire. Place two flat beads at the bottom and glue acrylic stone flower to flat beads. Shape beaded wire into a wavy shape and attach at back of butterfly with a staple or heavy tape.

SUPPLIES

Large Wood Butterfly Cut-Out
(Our butterfly came with wire antennae)

Gesso

Sandpaper and Tack Cloth

Acrylic Craft Paints — Americana® Royal Fuchsia; Delta Ceramcoat® Bubble Gum; DecoArt® Dazzling Metallics® Festive Green

Assorted Paintbrushes

Green Card Stock*

Scrapbook Paper*

Paper Craft Glue

Foam Mounting Tape

Heavy-Guage Wire

Assorted Pink, Lavendar, and Green Beads

Clear Bead Glue

Flower-Shaped and Round Peel & Stick Acrylic Stones

Stapler or Heavy Tape

*Debbie Mumm® scrapbook products are available at Jo-Ann Fabric and Craft Stores.

Girl
STUFF

What's pink and green and oh so pretty? Little ladies love feminine accessories in their rooms and this lamp and jewel box hit the mark perfectly. A bright striped fabric dresses the lamp shade and jewel box with gorgeous pattern and color.

SUPPLIES

Pink Lucite Lamp Base*

Drum Shade to fit Lamp (Ours is 8½" tall; 6½" top circumference; 7" bottom circumference)

Pink Fabric — 6" x 24" Strip

Stripe Fabric — 5" x 24" Strip

⅜" Pink Ribbon with Green Dots — 1¼ Yards

1" Green Grosgrain Ribbon — ⅔ yard

Clear Fabric Glue

Assorted Beads and Beading Wire

*Lamp shown was purchased at Jo-Ann Fabric and Craft Stores.

Making the Lamp

1. Sew pink and stripe fabric together along 24" length using ¼" seam allowance. Press seams open.

2. Wrap a piece of tracing paper around shade and using the side of the lead in a pencil, draw pencil along top edge and bottom edge of shade, making a pattern. Be sure to mark starting/ending point. Cut out paper pattern.

3. Lay pattern on sewn fabric from step 1. Drum shades may flare slightly at the bottom, making it difficult to keep fabric straight on shade. Pin pattern to sewn fabric, keeping seam line as even as possible. We chose to show 5" of pink and 3" of stripe. Cut fabric using pattern.

4. Using fabric glue, glue cut fabric to lamp shade and allow to dry. Cover seam line with 1" ribbon keeping ribbon straight with bottom edge. Ribbon will cover any unevenness of seam line caused by flare of shade.

5. Glue ⅜ " ribbon at top and bottom of shade to cover cut edges of fabric.

6. String assorted pink and green beads on wire and tie to lamp harp as an added accent.

Making the Jewel Box

1. Paint entire box with Gesso and allow to dry. Lightly sand and remove sanding residue with damp cloth.

2. Paint lid, base, and feet with Royal Fuchsia paint. Two or more coats may be needed for good coverage. Allow to dry thoroughly after each coat.

3. Referring to photo, measure part of box where fabric will be placed. Adhere fusible web to back of selected fabric, then cut fabric to measurement just taken, allowing a slight overlap in the back.

4. Using an appliqué iron, fuse fabric to box or glue in place.

5. String small beads on wire and place around base of box, securely twisting wire to secure in the back. Clip wire ends and place a drop of glue or clear fingernail polish over wire twist to avoid sharp ends.

6. Affix flower to top of box and use bead glue to glue on large bead.

SUPPLIES

Unfinished Wooden Box with Removable Lid*

Acrylic Craft Paint — Americana® Royal Fuchsia

Gesso, Assorted Paintbrushes, Fabric Scrap

Heavyweight Fusible Web

Small Pink and Green Beads and Wire

Flower-Shaped Peel & Stick Acrylic Stone

Large Pink Bead; Clear Bead Glue

*Our box came with ball feet, but if yours didn't and you like the look, purchase four ¾" wooden balls to glue to the base for feet.

FLUTTERBY HEADBOARD

Complete a sweet butterfly scene with a soft and cushy headboard decorated with flower buttons.* Use left-over fabric from the quilt, or purchase eight assorted fat quarters to make this easy project.

*Buttons are secured through several layers of fabric, but do not use if you think buttons will pose a choking hazard for your child.

Fabric Panels - *Eight Assorted Fat Quarters*
Refer to photo for fabric suggestions and cut the following from a variety of fabrics
   Four - 11½" squares
   Six - 9½" x 11½"
   Two - 9½" squares

Backing - 1¼ yards*

Batting
   Regular - 44" x 35"
   High Loft - 38" x 30"

Buttons - 15

Plywood - 30" x 38"

Staple Gun & Staples

*Fabric will not show

Getting Started

Soft puffy panels of this decorative headboard will complete a little girl's fresh room setting. Read all instructions before beginning and use ¼"-wide seam allowances.

Making the Fabric Panel

1. Refer to photo on page 47 for fabric color placement. Sew two 9½" x 11½" Fabric Panel pieces together along 11½" sides. Press. Sew this unit between two 11½" Fabric Panel squares. Press all seams in the same direction. Make two.

2. Sew two 9½" Fabric Panel squares together. Press. Sew this unit between two 9½" x 11½" Fabric Panel pieces. Press seams in opposite direction from rows in step 1.

3. Sew row from step 2 between two rows from step 1. Press.

4. Referring to Layering the Quilt on page 94, arrange and baste backing, regular batting, and top together. Stitch in the ditch.

5. Layer high-loft batting to back side of quilt unit. Sew buttons through all layers at panel intersections as desired; this will give extra dimension to headboard panel. If not using buttons, use heavy thread and a couple of overlapping stitches to "tuft" headboard at desired intersections. Trim backing and batting even with quilt top.

6. Center fabric panel unit on plywood. Pull sides of panel snugly over side edges of wood, checking to make sure panels are parallel to wood edge. Use staple gun to secure sides of quilted panel, working toward corners, stretching and checking placement. Repeat process for top and bottom edge.

7. Determine desired placement in room and attach headboard to wall using a wood cleat.

Lena - 2½ Years Old

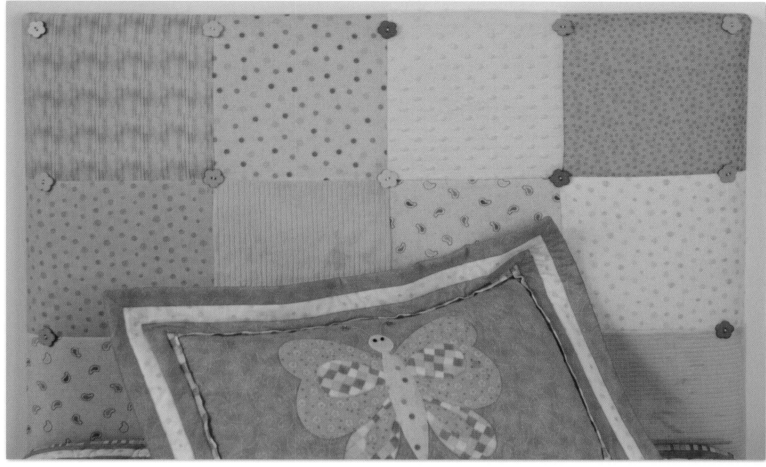

FLUTTERBY HEADBOARD Finished Size: 38" x 30"

Butterfly
PHOTO HOLDER

Your little princess will love helping you make this photo holder to display all her latest pictures. An over-sized wooden clothespin, scrapbook paper, and a sticker make this a fast and fun project

1. Take clothespin apart and paint wooden pieces with yellow paint. Two or more coats of paint may be needed for good coverage. Allow to dry thoroughly after each coat.

2. Following manufacturer's directions, apply gloss varnish to painted areas and allow to dry. Put clothespin back together.

3. Referring to photo, cut scrapbook paper to fit clothespin as shown. Glue paper to clothespin.

4. Invite your little girl to help place the sticker and the acrylic stones.

5. Matte a favorite photo using scrapbook paper and display by clipping it in the embellished clothespin.

Large Wooden Clothespin, Glue Stick
Yellow Acrylic Craft Paint
Assorted Paintbrushes, Gloss Varnish
Scrapbook Paper,* Butterfly Sticker*
Flower-Shaped and Round Peel & Stick Acrylic Stones
*Debbie Mumm® scrapbook products are available at Jo-Ann Fabric and Craft Stores.

Sugar & Spice Twin Bed Quilt Finished Size: 69" x 89"	FIRST CUT		SECOND CUT	
	Number of Strips or Pieces	Dimensions	Number of Pieces	Dimensions
Heart Block and Row				
Fabric A** Background ½ yard	1 2 1	5½" x 42" 3" x 42" 2½" x 42"	7 14 14	5½" squares 3" squares 2½" squares
Fabric B Hearts ¼ yard each of seven fabrics	1*	5½" x 42" *cut for each fabric	1* 2*	5½" squares 5" squares
Butterfly Block and Row				
Fabric A** Background ⅝ yard	2 1 2 2	3½" x 42" 3" x 42" 2½" x 42" 2" x 42"	12 6 6 24 6 5 2	3½" squares 3½" x 1½" 3" squares 2½" squares 2½" x 1½" 2" x 9½" 1¼" x 9½"
Fabric B Upper Butterfly Wing ¼ yard each of three fabrics	1*	4½" x 42" *cut for each fabric	4*	4½" x 7½"
Fabric C Lower Butterfly Wing ⅛ yard each of three fabrics	1*	3" x 42" *cut for each fabric	2* 4* 4*	3" squares 2½" x 4½" 2½" squares
Fabric D Butterfly Body ⅛ yard	1	1½" x 42"	6	1½" x 4½"
Flying Geese Row				
Fabric A** Background ½ yard	4	3½" x 42"	40 2	3½" squares 2" x 6½"
Fabric B Geese ¼ yard	2	3½" x 42"	10	3½" x 6½"
Fabric C Geese ⅙ yard	1	3½" x 42"	4	3½" x 6½"
Fabric D Geese ⅙ yard each of two fabrics	1*	3½" x 42" *cut for each fabric	3*	3½" x 6½"
Pinwheel Block and Row				
Fabric A** Background ⅜ yard	2	5½" x 42"	14	5½" squares
Fabric B Pinwheels ¼ yard each of seven fabrics	1*	5½" x 42" *cut for each fabric	2*	5½" squares

Sugar & Spice Twin Bed Quilt CONTINUED	FIRST CUT		SECOND CUT	
	Number of Strips or Pieces	Dimensions	Number of Pieces	Dimensions
Flower Block and Row				
Fabric A** Background ⅓ yard	2 3	2" x 42" 1½" x 42"	5 2 72	2" x 9½" 1¼" x 9" 1½" squares
Fabric B Flower ¼ yard each of three fabrics	1*	5" x 42" *cut for each fabric	8*	5" squares
Fabric C Appliqués Assorted Scraps				
Checkerboard Block and Row				
Fabric A Light Squares ½ yard	4	3½" x 42"		
Fabric B Medium Squares ¼ yard	2	3½" x 42"		
Fabric C Dark Squares ¼ yard	2	3½" x 42"		
Accent Strips and Borders				
First Accent Strip Repeating Stripe 1⅞ yards***	1 2 1 2	63½" x 5½" 63½" x 4½" 63½" x 3½" 63½" x 1½"		
Second Accent Strip ⅓ yard	5	1½" x 42"		
Third Accent Strip ¼ yard	2	2½" x 42"		
Fourth Accent Strip ¼ yard	2	3½" x 42"		
Fifth Accent Strip ⅓ yard	5	1½" x 42"		
First Border ⅓ yard	8	1" x 42"		
Outside Border ⅔ yard	8	2½" x 42"		
Binding ⅞ yard	9	2¾" x 42"		

Backing - 5½ yards
Batting - 77" x 97"
Lightweight Fusible Web - scraps

** If using one fabric for Fabric A total yardage needed is 2 yards.
***If using repeating stripe fabric adjust yardage to obtain the appropriate number of strips. Cut strips were cut lengthwise (parallel to selvage.)

Fabric Requirements and Cutting Instructions

Read all instructions before beginning and use ¼"-wide seam allowances throughout. Read Cutting Strips and Pieces on page 92 prior to cutting fabric pieces.

Getting Started

Butterflies, pinwheels, hearts and flowers are a few of the things girls love. Combine these elements with her favorite colors and your little girl will giggle with glee. Blocks measures 9½" square (unfinished). The quilt uses a repeating stripe for inspiration, color and use in accent strips. We used 6 different strip sections of various widths. Adjust your yardage if necessary. Refer to Accurate Seam Allowance on page 92. Whenever possible use the Assembly Line Method on page 92. Press seams in the direction of arrows.

Making the Heart Block and Row

1. Refer to Everything Nice Wall quilt pages 54-55 steps 1-5 to make a total of seven blocks using a different Fabric B for each heart. Refer to Twisting Seams on page 92. Press.

SUGAR & SPICE TWIN BED QUILT
Finished Size: 69" x 89"

She's sugar and spice and everything nice...and so is her quilt. This cute confection includes hearts, flowers, butterflies, and pinwheels, a whole row of each block, with checks and strips cut from a repeating stripe fabric pattern in between. You'll love the versatility of this design. Any 9" block can be substituted for one of the others and you can alter dimensions based on your repeating stripe. Have fun with this one!

2. Arrange and sew together seven Heart Blocks as shown. Press. Row measures 9½" x 63½".

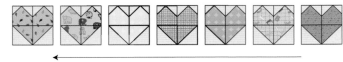

Row measures 9½" x 63½"

Making the Checkerboard Block and Row

1. Sew together lengthwise one 3½" x 42" Fabric B strip and one 3½" x 42" Fabric A strip to make a strip set. Press toward Fabric A. Make two. Cut strip set into twenty 3½"-wide segments as shown.

3½

Make 2
Cut 20 segments

2. Sew together lengthwise one 3½" x 42" Fabric C strip and one 3½" x 42" Fabric A strip to make a strip set. Press toward Fabric A. Make two. Cut strip set into twenty-two 3½"-wide segments, as shown.

3½

Make 2
Cut 22 segments

3. Sew two segments from step 1 together as shown. Press. Make four and label Unit 1. Sew together one segment from step 1 and one segment from step 2. Press. Make twelve and label Unit 2. Sew two segments from step 2 together. Press. Refer to Twisting Seams on page 92. Make four and label Unit 3.

Unit 1 **Unit 2** **Unit 3**

Make 4   Make 12   Make 4

SUGAR & SPICE TWIN BED QUILT Finished Size: 69" x 89"

4. Arrange and sew eight of Unit 2, one of Unit 1, one of Unit 3, and one segment from step 2 as shown. Press. Checkerboard Row 1 measures 6½" x 63½".

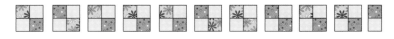

Row measures 6½" x 63½"

5. Arrange and sew four of Unit 2, three of Unit 1, three of Unit 3, and one segment from step 2 as shown. Press. Checkerboard Row 2 measures 6½" x 63½".

Row measures 6½" x 63½"

Making the Butterfly Block and Row

1. Draw a diagonal line on wrong side of one 3" Fabric A square. Place marked square and one 3" Fabric C square right sides together. Sew scant ¼" away from drawn line on both sides to make half-square triangles as shown. Make six, two of each combination. Cut on drawn line and press. Square to 2½". Make twelve half-square triangles, four of each combination.

Fabric A = 3 x 3   Square to 2½
Fabric C = 3 x 3   Make 12
Make 6   (four of each combination)
(two of each combination) Half-square Triangles

2. Refer to Quick Corner Triangles on page 92. Making quick corner triangle units, sew one unit from step 1 and one 3½" Fabric A square to one 4½" x 7½" Fabric B piece as shown. Press. Sew one matching 2½" Fabric C square to this unit as shown. Press. Make six, two of each fabric combination.

Unit from step 1
Fabric A = 3½ x 3½
Fabric C = 2½ x 2½
Fabric B = 4½ x 7½
Make 6
(two of each combination)

3. Making quick corner triangle units, sew one unit from step 1, one 3½" Fabric A square to one 4½" x 7½" Fabric B piece as shown. Press. Sew one matching 2½" Fabric C square to this unit as shown. Press. Make six, two of each fabric combination.

Unit from step 1
Fabric A = 3½ x 3½
Fabric C = 2½ x 2½
Fabric B = 4½ x 7½
Make 6
(two of each combination)

4. Sew one 3½" x 1½" Fabric A piece to one 1½" x 4½" Fabric D piece as shown. Press toward Fabric D. Make six. Sew this unit between one matching unit from step 2 and one unit from step 3 as shown. Press. Make six, two of each combination.

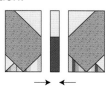

Make 6
(two of each combination)

5. Making quick corner triangle units sew two 2½" Fabric A squares to one 2½" x 4½" Fabric C piece as shown. Press. Make twenty-four, four of each fabric combination. Sew one 2½" x 1½" Fabric A piece between two of these matching units as shown. Press. Make six, two of each combination.

Fabric A = 2½ x 2½
Fabric C = 2½ x 4½
Make 12
(four of each combination)

1½
  2½

Make 6
(two of each combination)

6. Sew one unit from step 4 to one unit from step 5 matching fabric as shown. Press. Make six, two of each combination. Block measures 9½" square.

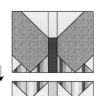

Make 6
(two of each combination)
Block measures 9½" square

7. Arrange and sew two 1¼" x 9½" Fabric A strips, six Butterfly Blocks, and five 2" x 9½" Fabric A strips as shown. Press. Row measures 9½" x 63½".

1¼   2   2   2   2   2   1¼

          9½

Row measures 9½" x 63½"

Making the Flying Geese Row

1. Refer to Quick Corner Triangles on page 92. Making quick corner triangle units, sew two 3½" Fabric A squares to one 3½" x 6½" Fabric B piece as shown. Press. Make ten.

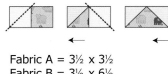

Fabric A = 3½ x 3½
Fabric B = 3½ x 6½
Make 10

2. Making quick corner triangle units, sew two 3½" Fabric A squares to one 3½" x 6½" Fabric C piece as shown. Press. Make four.

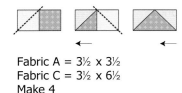

Fabric A = 3½ x 3½
Fabric C = 3½ x 6½
Make 4

3. Making quick corner triangle units, sew two 3½" Fabric A squares to one 3½" x 6½" Fabric D piece as shown. Press. Make six, three of each combination.

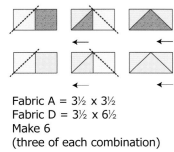

Fabric A = 3½ x 3½
Fabric D = 3½ x 6½
Make 6
(three of each combination)

4. Referring to photo on page 49 and diagram below, arrange and sew together ten assorted flying geese units. Press. Make two. Sew these rows together. Press.

5. Sew unit from step 4 between two 2" x 6½" Fabric A pieces. Press. Row measures 6½" x 63½".

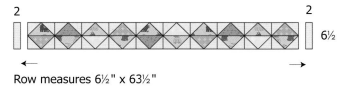

Row measures 6½" x 63½"

Making the Pinwheel Block and Row

Madison - 13 Months Old

1. Draw a diagonal line on wrong side of one 5½" Fabric A square. Place marked square and one 5½" Fabric B square right sides together. Sew scant ¼" away from drawn line on both sides to make half-square triangles as shown. Make fourteen, two of each fabric combination. Cut on drawn line and press. Square to 5". This will make twenty-eight half-square triangle units, four of each combination.

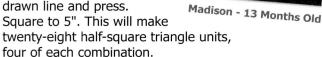

Fabric A = 5½ x 5½   Square to 5"
Fabric B = 5½ x 5½   Make 28
Make 14   Half-square Triangles
(2 of each combination)   (4 of each combination)

2. Sew two units from step 1 together as shown. Press. Make fourteen. Sew pairs together as shown. Refer to Twisting Seams on page 92. Press. Make seven, in assorted combinations. Block measures 9½" square.

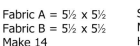

Make 14
(in assorted combinations)

Make 7
(in assorted combinations)
Block measure 9½" square

3. Arrange and sew together seven blocks from step 2. Press. Pinwheel Row measures 9½" x 63½".

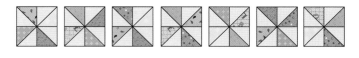

Row measures 9½" x 63½"

Making the Flower Block and Row

1. Refer to Quick Corner Triangles on page 92. Making quick corner triangle units, sew three 1½" Fabric A squares to one 5" Fabric B square as shown. Press. Make twenty-four, eight of each fabric combination.

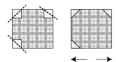

Fabric A = 1½ x 1½
Fabric B = 5 x 5
Make 24
(eight of each combination)

2. Sew two matching units from step 1 together as shown. Press. Make twelve, four of each combination. Sew two of these units together. Refer to Twisting Seams on page 92. Press. Make six, two of each combination. Repress Quick Corner Triangles as needed. Block measures 9½" square.

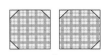

Make 12
(four of each combination)

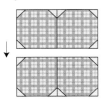

Make 6
(two of each combination)
Block measures 9½" square

3. Refer to appliqué instructions on page 93. Use patterns on page 95 to trace seven 2¾" and seven 2¼" circles on paper side of fusible web. Use appropriate fabrics to prepare all appliqués for fusing.

4. Refer to layout on page 50 to position and fuse appliqués to center of flower block. Finish appliqué edges with machine satin stitch or other decorative stitching as desired.

5. Arrange and sew two 1¼" x 9½" Fabric A strips, six Flower Blocks, and five 2" x 9½" Fabric A strips as shown. Press. Row measures 9½" x 63½".

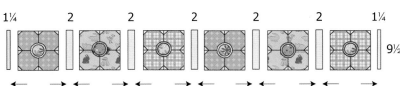

1¼ 2 2 2 2 2 1¼   9½

Row measures 9½" x 63½"

Assembling the Quilt

1. Sew 1½" x 42" Second Accent strips together end-to-end to make one continuous 1½"-wide Second Accent strip. Press. Cut three 1½" x 63½" Second Accent strips.

2. Sew 2½" x 42" Third Accent strips together end-to-end to make one continuous 2½"-wide Third Accent strip. Press. Cut one 2½" x 63½" Third Accent strip.

3. Repeat step 2 to sew 3½"-wide Fourth Accent strips and 1½"-wide Fifth Accent strips, end-to-end. Press. Cut one 3½" x 63½" Fourth Accent strip and three 1½" x 63½" Fifth Accent strips.

4. Referring to layout on page 50, arrange and sew together, 4½"-wide First Accent strip, Heart Row, one 1½"-wide Second Accent strip, Checkerboard Row 1, 1½"-wide Second Accent strip, Butterfly Row, 2½"-wide Third Accent strip, 3½"-wide First Accent strip, 1½"-wide Fifth Accent strip, Flying Geese Row, 1½"-wide Fifth Accent strip, 5½"-wide First Accent strip, 1½"-wide First Accent strip, Pinwheel Row, 1½"-wide First Accent strip, 3½"-wide Fourth Accent strip, Checkerboard Row 2, 1½"-wide Second Accent strip, 1½"-wide Fifth Accent strip, Flower Row, and 4½"-wide First Accent strip. Press.

5. Refer to Adding the Borders on page 94. Sew 1" x 42" First Border strips together end-to-end to make one continuous 1"-wide First Border strip. Measure quilt through center from side to side. Cut two 1"-wide First Border strips to this measurement. Sew to top and bottom of quilt. Press seams toward border.

6. Measure quilt through center from top to bottom including border just added. Cut two 1"-wide First Border strips to this measurement. Sew to sides of quilt. Press.

7. Refer to steps 5 and 6 to join, measure, trim, and sew 2½" Outside Border strips to top, bottom, and sides of quilt. Press.

Layering and Finishing

1. Cut backing crosswise into two equal pieces. Sew pieces together lengthwise to make one 98" x 80" (approximate) backing piece.

2. Referring to Layering the Quilt on page 94, arrange and baste backing, batting, and top together. Hand or machine quilt as desired.

3. Refer to Binding the Quilt on page 94. Sew 2¾" x 42" binding strips end-to-end to make one continuous 2¾"-wide binding strip. Bind quilt to finish.

EVERYTHING NICE WALL QUILT

Your little girl will giggle with delight with these multi-color hearts displayed on her wall. Blocks measure 9½" square (unfinished). Refer to Accurate Seam Allowance on page 92. Whenever possible use the Assembly Line Method on page 92. Press seams in the direction of arrows.

Making the Heart Block

1. Refer to Quick Corner Triangles on page 92. Making quick corner triangle units, sew one 2½" and one 3" Fabric A squares to one 5" Fabric B square as shown. Press. Make two, one of each variation.

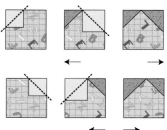

Fabric A = 2½ x 2½
          3 x 3
Fabric B = 5 x 5
Make 2
(one of each variation)

2. Sew units from step 1 together as shown. Press.

3. Draw a diagonal line on wrong side of one 5½" Fabric A square. Place marked square and one 5½" Fabric B square right sides together. Sew scant ¼" away from drawn line on both sides to make half-square triangles as shown. Cut on drawn line and press. Square to 5". This will make two half-square triangle units.

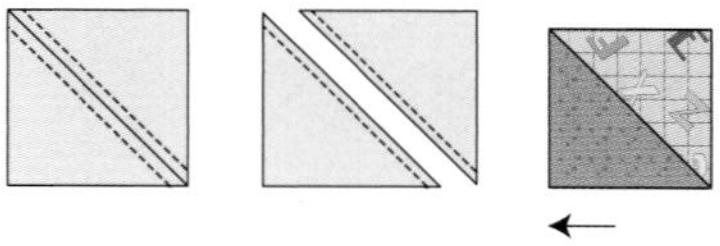

Fabric A = 5½ x 5½   Square to 5"
Fabric B = 5½ x 5½   Make 2
                          Half-square Triangles

4. Sew units from step 3 together as shown. Press.

Fabric Requirements and Cutting Instructions

Read all instructions before beginning and use ¼"-wide seam allowances throughout. Read Cutting Strips and Pieces on page 92 prior to cutting fabric.

Everything Nice Wall Quilt Finished Size: 36½" x 36½"	FIRST CUT	
	Number of Strips or Pieces	Dimensions
Fabric A Background ¼ yard each of nine fabrics** Note: We elected to repeat two fabrics	1* 2* 2*	5½" square 3" squares 2½" squares *cut for each fabric
Fabric B Heart ¼ yard each of nine fabrics** Note: We elected to repeat one fabric	1* 2*	5½" square 5" squares *cut for each fabric
First Border ⅙ yard	2 2	1" x 28½" 1" x 27½"
Second Border ¼ yard	2 2	1¼" x 30" 1¼" x 28½"
Outside Border ½ yard	2 2	3½" x 36" 3½" x 30"
Binding ⅜ yard	4	2¾" x 42"
Backing - 1⅛ yards Batting - 40" x 40" **If using the same fabric for Fabrics A and B, one ¼ yard cut of fabric is enough.		

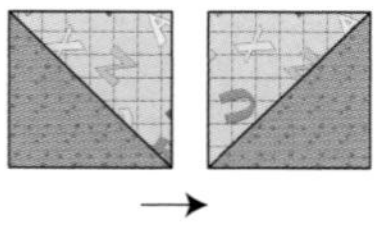

5. Sew unit from step 2 to unit from step 4 together as shown. Refer to Twisting Seams on page 92. Press. Block measures 9½" square.

Block measures 9½" square

6. Repeat steps 1-5 to make a total of nine blocks in different color combinations.

Assembly

1. Refer to photo to arrange blocks in three rows with three blocks each. Sew blocks together pressing seams in opposite direction from row to row. Sew rows together. Press.

2. Sew quilt top between two 1" x 27½" First Border strips. Press seams toward border. Sew quilt between two 1" x 28½" First Border strips. Press.

3. Sew quilt between two 1¼" x 28½" Second Border strips. Press seams toward border. Sew quilt between two 1¼" x 30" Second Border strips. Press.

4. Sew quilt between two 3½" x 30" Outside Border strips. Press toward border. Sew quilt between two 3½" x 36" Outside Border strips. Press.

Layering and Finishing

1. Referring to Layering the Quilt on page 94, arrange and baste backing, batting, and top together. Hand or machine quilt as desired.

2. Refer to Binding the Quilt on page 94 and using 2¾"-wide strips, bind quilt to finish.

EVERYTHING NICE WALL QUILT
Finished Size: 36½" x 36½"

Here's my heart, and Daddy's, Grannie's, and Sissy's too! Your Little Heartbreaker will love this eye-catching wall quilt filled with her favorite heart shape in the same luscious colors as the bed quilt. A playful polka-dot border and binding provide the perfect finish.

SUGAR & SPICE PILLOW

Sugar & Spice Pillow Finished Size: 21½" square	FIRST CUT	
	Number of Strips or Pieces	Dimensions
Fabric A Background ⅓ yard	1	5½" square
	2	3" squares
	2	2½" x 13½"
	2	2½" x 9½"
	2	2½" squares
Fabric B Heart ¼ yard	1	5½" square
	2	5" squares
Fabric C Accent Border ⅛ yard	2	1¼" x 15"
	2	1¼" x 13½"
Fabric D Outside Border ⅓ yard	2	4" x 22"
	2	4" x 15"
Backing ⅔ yard	2	22" x 13¾"

Lining - ⅔ yard
Batting - 24" x 24"
Pillow Form - 13" or 21½"
Pillow Form Fabric (Optional) - ½ yard or ⅔ yard
    Two 15" Squares or Two 22" squares
Polyester Fiberfill (Optional)

Dress-up isn't complete without all the accessories! The same is true for her bedroom and a heart pillow is the crowning touch for her princess palace.

Making the Heart Block

1. Refer to Everything Nice Wall Quilt, Heart Block instructions, on pages 54-55 to make one Heart Block.

2. Sew block between two 2½" x 9½" Fabric A pieces. Press away from center. Sew this unit between two 2½" x 13½" Fabric A pieces. Press.

Finishing the Pillow

1. Sew heart square between two 1¼" x 13½" Fabric C strips. Press toward Fabric C. Sew this unit between two 1¼" x 15" Fabric C strips. Press.

2. Sew unit from step 1 between two 4" x 15" Fabric D strips. Press toward Fabric D. Sew this unit between two 4" x 22" Fabric D strips. Press.

3. Referring to Finishing Pillows on page 95, step 1, to prepare pillow top for quilting. Quilt as desired.

4. Use two 13¾" x 22" backing pieces and refer to Finishing Pillows, page 95, steps 2-4, to sew backing. Note: If a smaller pillow with flange is desired, stitch-in-the-ditch between accent border and outside border. Insert 14½" pillow form or 21½" pillow form or refer to Pillow Forms page 95 to make a pillow form if desired.

Kate - 1 Year Old

Sugar & Spice
LAMP

Cuddle up on the bed and turn on the light for the nightly ritual of story time. With a lamp this lovely you'll want to linger, watching the golden glow highlighting all the dainty details of the lamp and shade.

Making the Lamp

1. Refer to General Painting Directions on page 95. If needed, sand lamp base to remove gloss and use a damp cloth to remove residue.

2. Using details of lamp base as a guide, determine placement of each color. Paint the largest section first; two or more coats of paint may be needed for good coverage. Always allow paint to dry thoroughly after each coat. Continue adding paint colors, one at a time, using a fine paintbrush to define edges of each stripe.

3. When completed and thoroughly dry, apply gloss varnish for shine and durability.

4. To embellish the shade, use a tape measure to determine the length needed for trim pieces, adding 1" to wrap to the inside.

5. Mark the vertical center of shade, and using fabric glue at top and bottom of the shade, stretch center trim piece in center of shade. Add a bit more glue at the top and bottom back to secure trim. We used small office binder clips to hold the ribbon in place while glue sets. Continue adding trim in this way until sides of shade are complete. Glue rickrack along bottom of shade to complete the embellishment.

Lamp Base (Ours was plain white originally)

Lamp Shade (Ours is 9" high and 36" around the bottom)

Acrylic Craft Paints — FolkArt® Baby Pink and Warm White; Americana® Moon Yellow and Royal Fuchsia; Delta Ceramcoat® Bubble Gum and Pansy

Gloss Varnish

Assorted Paintbrushes

Sandpaper

Assorted Trims for Shade — Amount depends on the shade
We used: Pink Metallic RickRack: 3⅛ yards
Dark Pink Dotted Ribbon: 2¼ yards
Yellow/Pink Floral Ribbon: 1⅛ yards

Clear-Drying Fabric Glue

ALL BOY

Little boys love cars and toys, frogs, dirt, and lots of noise!

Richard - 6½ Years Old,
Brandon - 2½ Years Old

Little boy adventures begin with a room as imaginative and clever as he is. Whether he loves moving things or turtles, frogs, and snails he'll find a world of imaginative play right on top of his bed!

Gabriel Brian - 1½ Years Old

ROAD RALLY TWIN BED QUILT

Getting Started

Cars and trucks are a boy's favorite toys so make this quilt for your little racecar superstar. With its interplay of tire tracks and pinwheel stars this quilt is a rally winner. Blocks measure 8½" square (unfinished). Refer to Accurate Seam Allowance on page 92. Whenever possible use the Assembly Line Method on page 92. Press seams in the direction of arrows.

Making the Block

Use lights, mediums and darks in the same colorway to make blocks.

1. Sew together lengthwise one 2½" x 42" Fabric B strip and one 1½" x 42" Fabric D strip. Press seam toward Fabric B. Make two. Cut strip sets into forty 1½"-wide segments as shown.

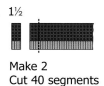

1½

Make 2
Cut 40 segments

2. Arrange and sew two units from step 1 and one 2½" x 1½" Fabric B piece as shown. Press. Make twenty.

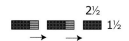

2½

1½

Make 20

3. Sew one unit from step 2 between two 2½" x 8½" Fabric D pieces as shown. Press. Make twenty.

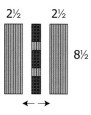

2½   2½

8½

Make 20

Fabric Requirements and Cutting Instructions

Road Rally Twin Bed Quilt Finished Size: 75 x 93"	FIRST CUT		SECOND CUT	
	Number of Strips or Pieces	Dimensions	Number of Pieces	Dimensions
Fabric A Background ⅞ yard	8	3½" x 42"	80	3½" squares
Fabric B Block Dark ⅝ yard each of four fabrics	3* 3*	3½" x 42" 2½" x 42" *cut for each fabric	20* 20*	3½" x 5½" 2½" x 1½"
Fabric C Block Medium ¼ yard each of four fabrics	2*	3½" x 42" *cut for each fabric	20*	3½" squares
Fabric D Block Light ⅞ yard each of four fabrics	10* 2*	2½" x 42" 1½" x 42" *cut for each fabric	40*	2½" x 8½"
Fabric E Lattice & Border 1⅞ yards	25	2½" x 42"	31	2½" x 16½"
Fabric F Accent Squares ⅛ yard	1	2½" x 42"	12	2½" squares
Binding ⅞ yard	9	2¾" x 42"		
Backing - 7 yards Batting - 83" x 101"				

Read all instructions before beginning and use ¼"-wide seam allowances throughout. Read Cutting Strips and Pieces on page 92 prior to cutting fabric.

4. Refer to Quick Corner Triangles on page 92. Making a quick corner triangle unit, sew one 3½" Fabric A square to one 3½" x 5½" Fabric B piece as shown. Press. Make twenty.

Fabric A = 3½ x 3½
Fabric B = 3½ x 5½
Make 20

5. Sew one 3½" Fabric C square to one unit from step 4 as shown. Press. Make twenty.

3½

3½

Make 20

6. Sew one unit from step 3 to one unit from step 5 as shown. Press. Make twenty and label Unit 1.

Unit 1

Make 20

7. Referring to steps 1-6 arrange and sew lights, mediums, and darks in each colorway to make twenty each of Unit 2, Unit 3, and Unit 4.

Unit 2   **Unit 3**   **Unit 4**

Make 20   Make 20   Make 20

ROAD RALLY TWIN BED QUILT
Finished Size: 75" x 93"

A little boy will drive off to Dreamland when tucked under this colorful quilt. During the day, he'll want to play, driving his cars on sashing roads to the next pinwheel neighborhood.

8. Sew one Unit 1 to one Unit 2, noting orientation of units. Press. Sew one Unit 3 to one Unit 4, noting orientation of units. Press. Arrange and sew units together as shown. Press. Make twenty. Block measures 16½" square.

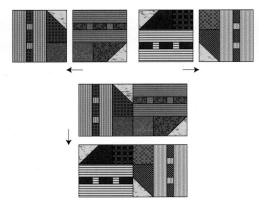

Make 20
Block measures 16½" square

Assembling the Quilt

1. Referring to photo on page 61 and layout, arrange all blocks checking orientation prior to sewing. Sew together four blocks and three 2½" x 16½" Fabric E strips. Press seams toward Fabric B. Make five rows.

2. Referring to photo on page 61 and layout, arrange and sew together four 2½" x 16½" Fabric E strips and three 2½" Fabric F squares. Press toward Fabric E. Make four.

3. Referring to photo on page 61 and layout, arrange and sew rows from step 1 and 2 together alternating rows. Press.

4. Refer to Adding the Borders on page 94. Sew 2½" x 42" Fabric E strips together end-to-end to make one continuous 2½"-wide Fabric E strip. Measure quilt through center from side to side. Cut two 2½"-wide Fabric E strips to this measurement. Sew to top and bottom of quilt. Press seams toward border.

5. Measure quilt through center from top to bottom including border just added. Cut two 2½"-wide Fabric E strips to this measurement. Sew to sides of quilt. Press.

ROAD RALLY TWIN BED QUILT Finished Size: 75" x 93"

Layering and Finishing

1. Cut backing crosswise into three equal pieces. Sew pieces together lengthwise to make one 84" x 120" (approximate) backing piece. Press and trim to 84" x 101".

2. Refer to Layering the Quilt on page 94 to arrange and baste backing, batting, and top together. Hand or machine quilt as desired.

3. Refer to Binding the Quilt on page 94. Sew 2¾" x 42" binding strips end-to-end to make one continuous 2¾"-wide binding strip. Bind quilt to finish.

Road Rally
LETTERS

SUPPLIES

8" Papier-mâché Letters to Spell Child's Name

Dimensional Unfinished Wooden Car (Optional)

Gesso

Assorted Paintbrushes

8½" x 11" Stencils - **Checks, repeating rectangles, diagonal lines, horizontal lines**

Stenciling Sponge

Circles Template

Acrylic Craft Paints — **Delta Ceramcoat® in Crocus Yellow, Leaf Green, Opaque Red, Navy Blue, and Blue Bayou. Americana® in Golden Straw, or colors of your choice.**

Sawtooth Picture Hangers

1. Refer to General Painting Directions on page 95 before beginning this project.

2. Apply Gesso to each letter and car cutout and allow to dry. Gesso prepares the surface for painting and is especially important when working with papier-mâché products.

3. Base coat each letter in the color of your choice. Two or more coats of paint may be needed for good coverage. Allow paint to dry thoroughly after each application of paint.

4. Place selected stencil on first letter and hold in place with fingertips. Dip sponge in a contrasting paint color, blot several times on a paper towel, then using an up and down tapping motion, apply paint to stencil. Carefully remove stencil and allow paint to dry. If needed for coverage, reposition stencil and repeat process until design is complete. Carefully clean stencil using warm water and dry flat on a paper towel. Repeat process using a different stencil for each letter.

Tip: Many stencils have prepunched holes on one side which can be stored in a binder to keep them flat, in order, and to allow for easy selection. Stencils without punched holes can be stored in binder pockets.

5. For the letter featuring circles, use a circles template and a pencil to draw a variety of circles on the letter and inside other circles. Using small brushes and all the paint colors, paint circles as desired using photo as inspiration.

6. If desired, paint car using directions on page 69, and glue to one letter as an accent.

7. Hang letters on wall using sawtooth picture hangers.

Any little boy would love to see his name in these bright and bold letters! Stencils make it easy to create racy letters perfect for a transportation-themed room.

LET'S GO ORGANIZER

Fabric Requirements and Cutting Instructions

Read all instructions before beginning and use ¼"-wide seam allowances throughout. Read Cutting Strips and Pieces on page 92 prior to cutting fabric.

Let's Go Organizer Finished Size: 30" x 31"	FIRST CUT		SECOND CUT	
	Number of Strips or Pieces	Dimensions	Number of Pieces	Dimensions
Fabric A Background 1¼ yards	2 6 2 1	10½" x 42" 2½" x 42" 2" x 42" 1½" x 42" (strip set)	2 2 4 2 3	10½" x 25½" 2½" x 30½" 2½" x 25½" 2" x 25½" 1½" squares
Fabric B Accent ⅛ yard	1	2½" x 42" (strip set)		
Fabric C Large Pocket Trim ½ yard each of two fabrics	1*	13" x 8½" *cut for each fabric		
Fabric D Large Pocket ½ yard each of two fabrics	1*	13" x 6½" *cut for each fabric		
Fabric E Medium Pocket Trim ⅓ yard	1	8½" x 10"		
Fabric F Medium Pocket ⅓ yard	1	10" x 6½"		
Fabric G Small Pocket Trim ⅓ yard each of two fabrics	1*	8¼" x 8½" *cut for each fabric		
Fabric H Small Pocket ¼ yard each of two fabrics	1*	6½" x 8¼" *cut for each fabric		
Binding ⅜ yard	4	2¾" x 42"		

Appliqués - Assorted Scraps
Backing - 1 yard
Batting - 34" x 35", two 25½" x 7¼"
Lightweight Fusible Web - ½ yard

Getting Started

Little cars underfoot? This great organizer is a sure way to inspire your son to pick up those small cars and trucks. Whenever possible use the Assembly Line Method on page 92. Press seams in the direction of arrows.

Making the Organizer

1. Sew together lengthwise 2½" x 42" Fabric B strip and 1½" x 42" Fabric A strip to make a strip set. Press seam toward Fabric B. Cut strip set into twenty-four 1½"-wide segments as shown.

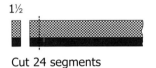

1½

Cut 24 segments

2. Sew together eight segments from step 1 and one 1½" Fabric A square as shown. Press. Make three.

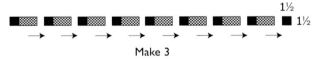

1½
1½

Make 3

3. Arrange and sew together two 2" x 25½" Fabric A strips, three units from step 2, and two 10½" x 25½" Fabric A strips, as shown. Press.

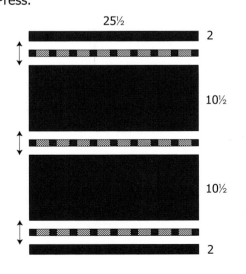

25½
2
10½
10½
2

Adding the Borders

1. Sew two 2½" x 25½" Fabric A pieces to top and bottom of quilt. Press.

2. Sew two 2½" x 30½" Fabric A pieces to sides of quilt.

Layering and Finishing

1. Referring to Layering the Quilt on page 94, arrange and baste backing, batting, and top together. Hand or machine quilt as desired.

2. Press four 2¾" binding strips in half, wrong sides together. Refer to Binding the Quilt on page 94 and bind quilt to finish.

Making the Pockets

1. Sew one 13" x 8½" Fabric C piece to one 13" x 6½" Fabric D piece. Press seams in opposing directions. Make two, one of each combination.

2. Sew two units from step 1 together as shown. Refer to Twisting Seams on page 92. Press.

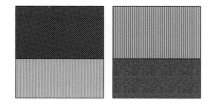

3. Sew 8½" x 10" Fabric E piece to 10" x 6½" Fabric F piece. Press seam toward Fabric E.

4. Sew one 8¼" x 8½" Fabric G piece to one 6½" x 8¼" Fabric H piece. Press seam toward Fabric H. Make two.

5. Sew unit from step 3 between two units from step 4. Twist seams. Press and label bottom pocket.

LET'S GO ORGANIZER
Finished Size: 30" x 31"

Zoom Zoom Zoom! It's a race to the finish when it comes to car and truck pick up! This cool organizer serves as both wall décor and a storage space for his favorite tiny toys.

Adding the Appliqués

Refer to appliqué instructions on page 93. Our instructions are for Quick-Fuse Appliqué, but if you prefer hand appliqué, reverse templates and add ¼"-wide seam allowances.

1. Use patterns on pages 67 and 68 to trace cars and trucks on paper side of fusible web. Use appropriate fabrics to prepare all appliqués for fusing.

2. Refer to photo on page 65 and layout to position and fuse appliqués to pocket sections. Finish appliqué edges with machine satin stitch or other decorative stitching as desired.

Finishing the Organizer

1. Fold top pocket right sides together and layer with batting. Stitch side seams only. Clip corners, turn right side out, and press. Repeat for bottom pocket.

2. Quilt pocket as desired.

3. Refer to photo on page 65, layout and diagram below. Determine top pocket placement. Bottom of pocket should align with seam line of organizer background. Place pocket, right side down, on organizer and stitch a scant ¼" away from raw edge. Fold pocket up toward top of organizer and pin in place. Stitch in-the-ditch between pocket sections then ¼" away from seam on both sides. Edge stitch bottom and side edges in place and stitch again ¼" from stitch line.

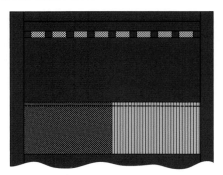

4. Repeat step 3 for bottom pocket section.

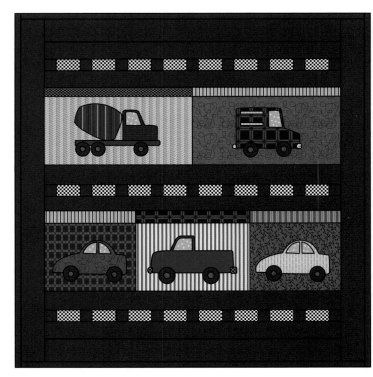

LET'S GO ORGANIZER Finished Size: 30" x 31"

Gavin - 6 Months Old

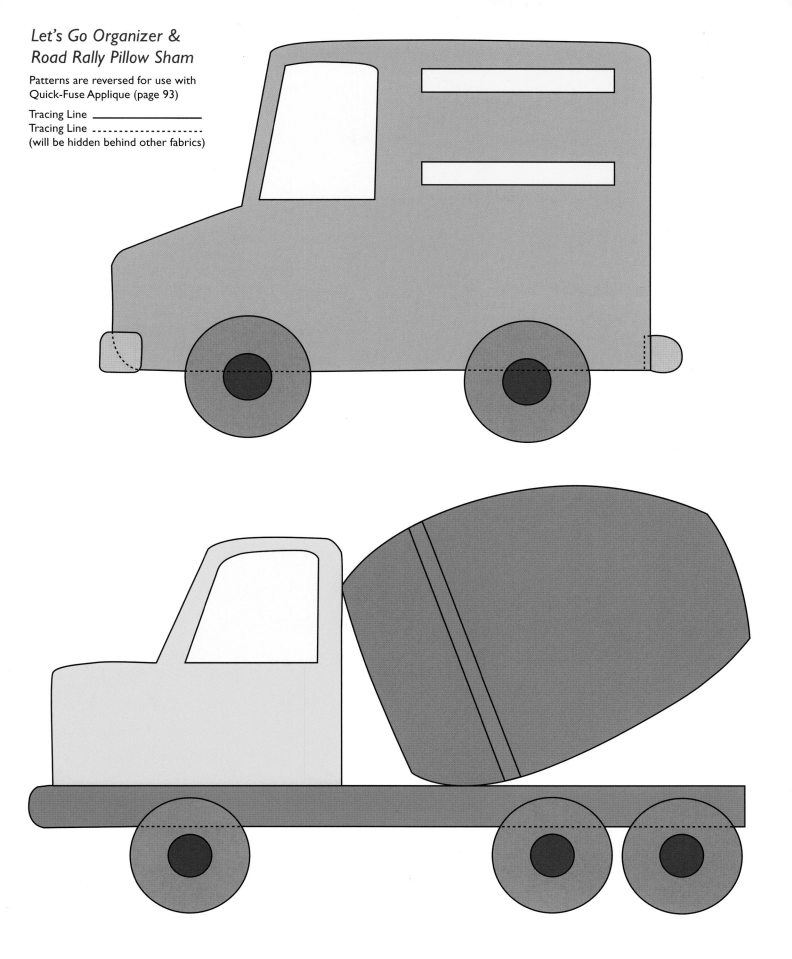

Let's Go Organizer &
Road Rally Pillow Sham

Patterns are reversed for use with
Quick-Fuse Applique (page 93)

Tracing Line ————————
Tracing Line - - - - - - - - - - - - - - - -
(will be hidden behind other fabrics)

Let's Go Organizer &
Road Rally Pillow Sham

Patterns are reversed for use with
Quick-Fuse Applique (page 93)

Tracing Line ——————
Tracing Line - - - - - - - - - -
(will be hidden behind other fabrics)

Permission is granted by Debbie Mumm Inc.
to copy page 64 to successfully complete project.

Beep Beep
TOY CHEST

Unfinished Bench-Style Toy Chest

Sandpaper

Water-Based Primer

Large Bottles Acrylic Craft Paints
Delta Ceramcoat® Navy Blue and Opaque Red

Small Bottles Acrylic Craft Paints
Americana® Moon Yellow, Leaf Green,
Light Buttermilk, and Black

DecoArt® No Prep Metal Paint
Bright Silver

Assorted Paintbrushes*

Water-Based Matte Varnish

Tacky Craft Glue

Small Unfinished Dimensional Wood Car

**Small Wood Letters to Spell
"Beep Beep" or Your Choice of Words**

*2" foam or bristle brush is handy when basecoating large areas such as the lower part of toy box.

Painting the Toy Box

1. Refer to General Painting Directions on page 95. Lightly sand toy box and use a damp cloth to remove sanding residue.

2. Apply primer to toy box and small wooden car and allow to dry thoroughly. Lightly sand any spots where primer is uneven and remove residue with damp cloth.

3. Basecoat bottom of toy box using Navy Blue Paint. When basecoating, two or more coats of paint may be needed for good coverage. Always allow paint to dry thoroughly between coats of paint and clean brush with soap and water.

4. Basecoat seat of toy box and small wooden letters with Opaque Red. Allow to dry.

5. Basecoat back of toy box with Moon Yellow. When thoroughly dry, paint spindles Opaque Red, Leaf Green, and Navy Blue. Allow to dry.

Painting the Car

1. Paint body of the car with Leaf Green and allow to dry. Mix a small amount of Light Buttermilk with Leaf Green and paint fenders with this lighter green.

2. Paint windows with Light Buttermilk and allow to dry. Mix a small amount of Navy Blue into Light Buttermilk paint and use a fan brush to add texture to the windows as shown in photo.

3. Paint tires with Black paint.

4. Paint hubcaps and bumpers with silver paint. When dry, use black paint to add details to hubcaps as shown in photo.

5. Paint taillight with Opaque Red. Add other details as desired.

Finishing the Toy Box

1. Use tacky glue to adhere letters and car to back of toy box and allow to dry.

2. Following manufacturer's directions, apply varnish to all painted surfaces of toy box. Allow to dry.

Cute and convenient, this toy chest is decorative, useful, and serves as seating for a little boy's room. Primary colors and easy painting techniques make this a fast and fun project; and small wooden letters and a racy car shift this project into high gear.

ROAD RALLY
PILLOW SHAM

Road Rally Pillow Sham Finished Size: 20" x 26"	FIRST CUT		SECOND CUT	
	Number of Strips or Pieces	Dimensions	Number of Pieces	Dimensions
Fabric A Background & Backing 1⅛ yard	1	20½" x 42"	1	20½" square
			1	20½" x 11½"
	2	7" x 42"	2	7" x 26½"
	1	1½" x 42"		
	2	1" x 42"	2	1" x 26½"
Fabric B Tire Tracks ⅛ yard	1	2½" x 42"		
Fabric C Appliqué Background ⅙ yard	1	4½" x 42"	1	4½" x 26½"
Appliqués - Assorted Scraps Batting - 24" x 30" Lightweight Fusible Web - ¼ yard				

Fabric Requirements and Cutting Instructions

Read all instructions before beginning and use ¼"-wide seam allowances throughout. Read Cutting Strips and Pieces on page 92 prior to cutting fabric.

Getting Started

This easy to make pillow sham with its crayon colored vehicles will bring delight to your young son's bed. Refer to Accurate Seam Allowance on page 92 and whenever possible use the Assembly Line Method on page 92. Press seams in the direction of arrows.

Making the Sham

1. Cut two 2½" x 1½" pieces from 2½" x 42" Fabric B strip, set aside until step 2. Sew together lengthwise remainder 2½"-wide Fabric B strip and 1½" x 42" Fabric A strip. Press towards Fabric B. Cut strip set into sixteen 1½"-wide segments as shown.

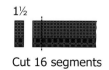

1½

Cut 16 segments

2. Arrange and sew together eight segments from step 1 and one 2½" x 1½" Fabric B piece as shown. Press. Make two.

2½ 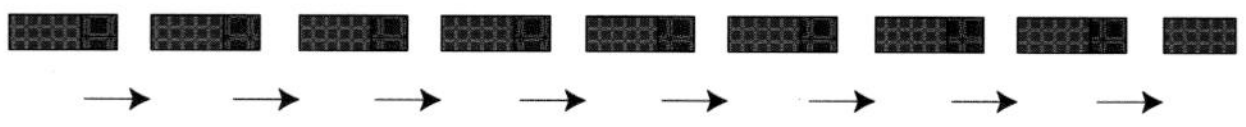
1½

Make 2

3. Sew one 4½" x 26½" Fabric C strip between two 1" x 26½" Fabric A strips. Press seams toward Fabric C.

4. Referring to photo, sew unit from step 3 between two units from step 2. Press seams toward center.

5. Sew unit from step 4 between two 7" x 26½" Fabric A pieces. Press seams toward Fabric A.

6. Use patterns on page 64 to trace car and truck patterns on paper side of fusible web. Use appropriate fabrics to prepare all appliqués for fusing.

7. Refer to photo to position and fuse appliqués to Fabric C strip. Finish appliqué edges with machine satin stitch or other decorative stitching as desired.

8. Referring to Finishing Pillows on page 95, step 1, to prepare pillow top for quilting. Quilt as desired.

9. Use one 20½" square and one 20½" x 11½" backing piece and refer to Finishing Pillows, page 95, steps 2-4, to sew backing. Turn, press, and insert standard pillow.

Cars and a truck hurry on their merry way to fulfilling a small boy's dreams. Easy piecing and cute appliqués make this project fast and fun.

Road Rally
LAMP

Colorful cars race around the track on this cute bedside lamp. Simple painting and fabric appliqués shift a plain lamp into gear for a boisterous young boy.

Painting the Lamp

1. Sand lamp base to remove shine and oils. Use a damp cloth to remove residue.

2. Basecoat shaft of lamp with Linen paint. When basecoating, two or more coats of paint may be needed for good coverage. Allow paint to dry thoroughly between coats and clean paintbrushes with soap and water. Allow to dry.

3. Basecoat base with Navy Blue Paint. Allow to dry.

4. Using features on your lamp and photo as inspiration, determine placement of Opaque Red and Leaf Green paint. Paint as desired. Allow to dry.

5. Following manufacturer's directions, apply matte varnish.

Making the Lampshade

Refer to Quick-Fuse Applique and Applique Pressing Sheet on page 93. Reduce pattern by 50% on page 68, prepare eight car appliqués. Use craft glue to adhere appliqués to lampshade.

Lamp Base

Lampshade*

Sandpaper

Assorted Paintbrushes

Acrylic Craft Paints — **Delta Ceramcoat®**
Navy Blue and Opaque Red;
Americana® Leaf Green; FolkArt® Linen

Matte Spray Varnish

Assorted Fabrics for Appliqués

Lightweight Fusible Web - ¼ yard

Appliqué Pressing Sheet

Craft Glue

*Lampshade shown came with navy blue ribbon trim. If you want to add ribbon trim to a plain shade, use a cloth tape to measure the distance around the top and bottom of the shade and add a little extra for turning under.

Snips & Snails Wall or Crib Quilt Finished Size: 39 x 48"	FIRST CUT		SECOND CUT	
	Number of Strips or Pieces	Dimensions	Number of Pieces	Dimensions
Nine-Patch Block				
Fabric A ⅛ yard for 5 fabrics ¼ yard for 4 fabrics	1*	3½" x 42" *cut for each fabric		
	1**	3½" square** **cut 1 each from four fabrics		
Frog Block				
Fabric A Background ⅛ yard	1	2½" x 42"	4	2½" x 8½"
	1	1½" x 42"	4	1½" x 4½"
			2	1½" squares
			2	1" x 3½"
Fabric B Body ⅛ yard each of two fabrics	1*	3" x 3½"		
	1*	1½" x 42" *cut for each fabric	2*	1½" x 5½"
			2*	1½" x 2½"
			2*	1½" squares
Fabric C Chest ⅛ yard each of two fabrics	1*	3½" x 5½" *cut for each fabric		
Snail Block				
Fabric A Background ¼ yard	1	2½" x 42"	2	2½" x 6½"
	2	1½" x 42"	2	1½" x 7½"
			2	1½" x 6½"
			2	1½" x 2½"
			10	1½" squares
Fabric B Body ⅛ yard each of two fabrics	1*	1½" x 42" *cut for each fabric	1*	1½" x 8½"
			1*	1½" x 7½"
			1*	1½" x 2½"
			1*	1½" square
Fabric C Shell ¼ yard each of two fabrics	1*	6½" square *cut for each fabric		
Turtle Block				
Fabric A Background ¼ yard	1	2½" x 42"	2	2½" x 9½"
			4	2½" squares
	1	1½" x 42"	2	1½" x 9½"
			2	1½" x 6½"
			2	1½" x 2"
	1	1" x 42"	2	1" x 6½"
			4	1" x 2"
Fabric B Head, legs and tail ⅛ yard	1	1½" x 42"	8	1½" x 2"
Fabric C Shell ¼ yard	1	6½" x 42"	2	6½" squares

Snips & Snails Wall or Crib Quilt CONTINUED	FIRST CUT		SECOND CUT	
	Number of Strips or Pieces	Dimensions	Number of Pieces	Dimensions
Accent Border ¼ yard	5	1" x 42"	2	1" x 27½"
			4	1" x 3½"
Outside Border ½ yard	5	2½" x 42"		
Binding ½ yard	5	2¾" x 42"		
Appliqués - Assorted scraps Backing - 2⅜ yards Batting - 42½" x 52" Lightweight Fusible Web - ⅛ yard				

Fabric Requirements and Cutting Instructions

Read all instructions before beginning and use ¼"-wide seam allowances throughout. Read Cutting Strips and Pieces on page 92 prior to cutting fabric.

Getting Started

Any little boy would be delighted to receive this cute wall or crib quilt to decorate his room. This quilt consists of frog, snail, turtle and nine-patch blocks each measuring 9½" square (unfinished). Refer to Accurate Seam Allowance on page 92. Whenever possible use the Assembly Line Method on page 92. Press seams in the direction of arrows.

Making the Nine-Patch Blocks

1. Sew together lengthwise three different 3½" x 42" Fabric A strips to make a strip set. Make three, each using a different color combination. Press seams in opposite directions from set to set. Cut strip sets into thirty-two 3½"-wide segments as shown, eleven from each of two combinations and ten of one combination.

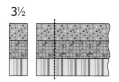

3½

Make 3
(1 of each combination)
Cut 32 segments
(11 of two combinations and
10 of one combination)

2. Arrange and sew together three strip sets from step 1 as shown, one of each combination. Press. Make six. Nine-Patch block measures 9½" square.

Make 6
Block measures 9½" square

3. Referring to photo and layout on page 74, arrange and sew together three segments from step 1 end-to-end to make top and bottom border units. Press. Make two. Set rows aside to use later in assembly of quilt top. (page 76, step 5)

4. Referring to photo and layout on page 74, arrange and sew together four units from step 1 end-to-end to make side border units. Press. Make two.

5. Referring to photo and layout on page 74, arrange and sew together two 3½" Fabric A squares, two 1" x 3½" Accent Border pieces and one unit from step 4. Press. Make two. Set rows aside to use later in assembly of quilt top for side-pieced borders. (page 76, step 7)

Making the Frog Block

1. Sew one 2½" x 8½" Fabric A strip to one 1½" x 2½" Fabric B piece as shown. Press. Make four, two of each combination.

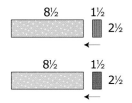

Make 4
(two of each combination)

SNIPS & SNAILS WALL OR CRIB QUILT
Finished Size: 39" x 48"

Snips and Snails, but no puppy dog tails! Your little one will love this colorful and crafty quilt featuring some of his favorite characters. Pieced turtles, frogs, and snails combine with nine-patch blocks to create a winsome wall or crib quilt.

2. Sew one 1½" x 4½" Fabric A piece to one 1½" x 5½" Fabric B piece as shown. Press. Make four, two of each combination.

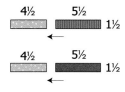

Make 4
(two of each combination)

3. Sew one 1½" Fabric A square between two matching 1½" Fabric B squares as shown. Press. Make two, one of each combination.

Make 2
(one of each combination)

4. Arrange and sew together one 1" x 3½" Fabric A piece, unit from step 3, one matching 3" x 3½" Fabric B piece and one 3½" x 5½" Fabric C piece as shown. Press. Make two, one of each combination.

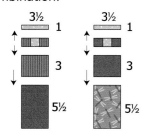

Make 2
(one of each combination)

5. Arrange and sew together matching units from steps 1, 2, and 4, as shown. Press. Make two, one of each combination. Frog Block measures 9½" square.

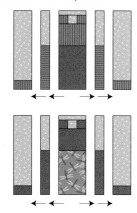

Make 2
(one of each combination)
Block measures 9½" square

Cuddle Quilts

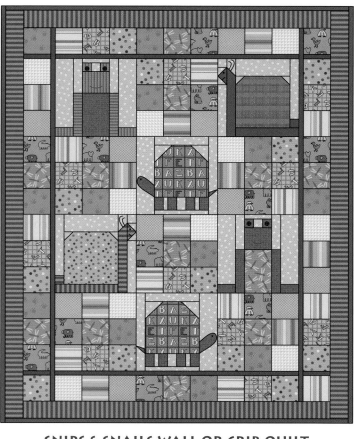

SNIPS & SNAILS WALL OR CRIB QUILT
Finished Size: 39" x 48"

6. Refer to appliqué instructions on page 93. Our instructions are for Quick-Fuse Appliqué, but if you prefer hand appliqué, add ¼"-wide seam allowances. Use patterns on page 77 to trace frog's eyes and mouth on paper side of fusible web. Use appropriate fabrics to prepare all appliqués for fusing.

7. Refer to photo on page 73 and layout to position and fuse appliqués to block. Finish appliqués edges with machine satin stitch or other decorative stitching as desired.

Making the Snail Block

1. Refer to Quick Corner Triangles on page 92. Making quick corner triangle units, sew two 1½" Fabric A squares to one 1½" x 2½" Fabric B piece as shown. Press. Make two, one of each combination.

Fabric A = 1½ x 1½
Fabric B = 1½ x 2½
Make 2
(one of each combination)

2. Sew one unit from step 1 between one 1½" Fabric A square and one 1½" x 6½" Fabric A piece as shown. Press. Make two, one of each variation and color combination.

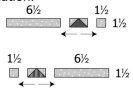

Make 2
(one of each variation & color combination)

3. Making a quick corner triangle unit, sew one 1½" x 2½" Fabric A piece to one 1½" x 8½" Fabric B strip, checking angle direction prior to sewing. Press. Make two, one of each variation and color combination.

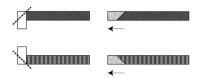

Fabric A =1½ x 2½
Fabric B= 1½ x 8½
Make 2
(one of each variation & color combination)

4. Making quick corner triangle units, sew two 1½" Fabric A squares to one 6½" Fabric C square as shown. Press. Make two, one of each combination.

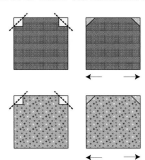

Fabric A = 1½ x 1½
Fabric C= 6½ x 6½
Make 2
(one of each combination)

5. Sew one unit from step 4 to one 2½" x 6½" Fabric A piece as shown. Press. Make two, one of each combination.

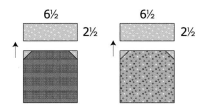

Make 2
(one of each combination

6. Sew one 1½" x 7½" Fabric A strip to one 1½" Fabric B square as shown. Press. Make two, one of each combination.

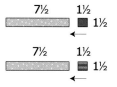

Make 2
(one of each combination)

7. Sew one unit from step 5 to one unit from step 6 as shown. Press. Make two, one of each variation and color combination.

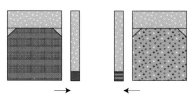

Make 2
(one of each variation & color combination)

8. Sew one unit from step 7 to one 1½" x 7½" Fabric B strip as shown. Press. Sew unit from step 3 between unit from step 2 and this unit as shown. Press. Make two, one of each variation and color combination. Snail Block measures 9½" square.

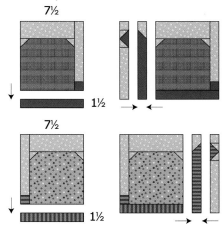

Make 2
(one of each variation & color combination)
Block measures 9½" square

9. Refer to appliqué instructions on page 93. Our instructions are for Quick-Fuse Appliqué, but if you prefer hand appliqué, add ¼"-wide seam allowances. Use eye pattern on page 77 to trace snail's eye on paper side of fusible web. Use appropriate fabric to prepare eye for fusing. Refer to photo on page 73 and layout on page 74 to position and fuse appliqués to blocks. Finish appliqué edges with machine satin stitch or other decorative stitching as desired.

10. Refer to snail placement guide on page 77 and trace eye and mouth placement to block. Hand or machine satin stitch, as desired.

Making the Turtle Block

1. Refer to Quick Corner Triangles on page 92. Making quick corner triangle units, sew two 2½" Fabric A squares to one 6½" Fabric C square as shown. Press. Make two.

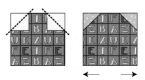

Fabric A = 2½ x 2½
Fabric C = 6½ x 6½
Make 2

2. Arrange and sew together four 1½" x 2" Fabric B pieces, two 1" x 2", and one 1½" x 2" Fabric A pieces as shown. Press. Sew to bottom of unit from step 1. Press. Make two.

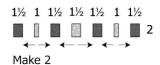

Make 2

3. Sew unit from step 2 between one 1½" x 6½" and one 1" x 6½" Fabric A strips. Press. Make two.

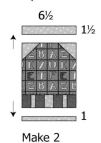

Make 2

4. Refer to appliqué instructions on page 93. Our instructions are for Quick-Fuse Appliqué, but if you prefer hand appliqué, reverse templates and add ¼"-wide seam allowance. Use patterns on page 77 to trace turtle's head, tail and eye on paper side of fusible web. Use appropriate fabrics to prepare all appliqués for fusing.

5. Refer to photo on page 73 and diagram below, to position and fuse turtle heads to 2½" x 9½" Fabric A strips and tails to 1½" x 9½" Fabric A strips. Finish appliqué edges with machine satin stitch or other decorative stitching as desired.

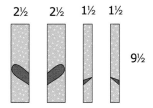

Appliqué one of each variation

6. Sew unit from step 3 between one of each appliqué units from step 5 as shown. Press. Make two, one of each variation. Turtle Block measures 9½" square.

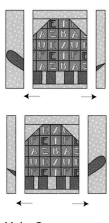

Make 2
(one of each variation)
Block measures 9½" square

Assembly

1. Referring to photo on page 73 and layout on page 74, arrange and sew one Nine-Patch Block between one Frog Block and one Snail Block. Press seams toward Nine-Patch Block. Make two, one of each variation.

2. Referring to photo on page 73 and layout on page 74, arrange and sew one Turtle Block between two Nine-Patch Blocks. Press seams toward Nine-Patch Block. Make two, one of each variation.

3. Arrange and sew together rows from steps 1 and 2. Press.

4. Sew quilt top between two 1" x 27½" Accent Border strips. Press seams toward border.

5. Referring to photo on page 73 and layout on page 74, sew quilt between top and bottom pieced borders. Press seams toward pieced border. (page 73, step 3)

6. Sew 1" x 42" Accent Border strips together end-to-end to make one continuous 1"-wide Accent Border strip. Measure quilt through center from top to bottom. Cut two 1"-wide Accent Border strips to this measurement. Sew to sides of quilt. Press seams toward border.

7. Referring to photo on page 73 and layout on page 74, sew quilt between two side-pieced borders. (page 73, step 5) Press seams toward pieced border.

8. Referring to Adding the Borders on page 94, sew 2½" x 42" Outside Border strips together end-to-end to make one continuous 2½"-wide Outside Border strip. Measure quilt through center from side to side. Cut two 2½"-wide Outside Border strips to this measurement and sew to top and bottom of quilt. Press seams toward border.

9. Measure quilt through center from top to bottom including border just added. Cut two 2½"-wide Outside Border strips to this measurement. Sew to sides of quilt. Press.

Layering and Finishing

1. Cut backing crosswise into two equal pieces. Sew pieces together lengthwise to make one 42½" x 80" (approximate) backing piece. Press and trim to 42½" x 52".

2. Referring to Layering the Quilt on page 94, arrange and baste backing, batting, and top together. Hand or machine quilt as desired.

3. Refer to Binding the Quilt on page 94. Sew 2¾" x 42" binding strips end-to-end to make one continuous 2¾"-wide binding strip. Bind quilt to finish.

Logan - 16 Months Old

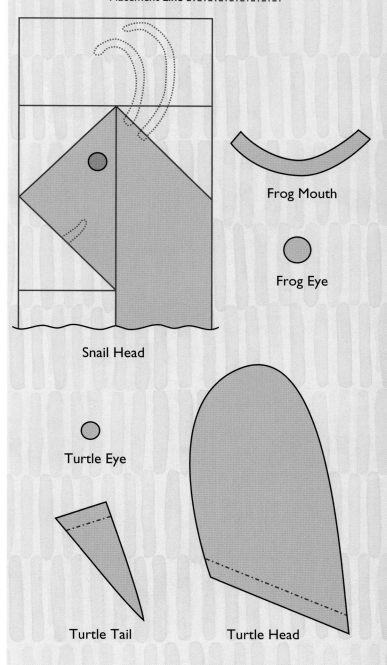

Snips & Snails Wall Quilt and Twin Bed Quilt

Patterns are reversed for use
with Quick-Fuse Applique (page 93)

Tracing Line _____
Embroidery Placement ....
Seam Line _____
Placement Line _._._._._._._._.

Frog Mouth

Frog Eye

Snail Head

Turtle Eye

Turtle Tail

Turtle Head

Snips & Snails Row Quilt Finished Size: 69 x 89"	FIRST CUT		SECOND CUT	
	Number of Strips or Pieces	Dimensions	Number of Pieces	Dimensions
Sailboat Block and Row				
Fabric A Background ⅝ yard**	1	4" x 42"	7	4" squares
	4	3½" x 42"	14	3½" x 6½"
			14	3½" squares
Fabric B Dark Boat Hull ⅛ yard	1	3½" x 42"	3	3½" x 9½"
Fabric C Light Boat Hull ⅛ yard	1	3½" x 42"	4	3½" x 9½"
Fabric D Sails ¼ yard	1	4" x 42"	3	4" squares
	1	3½" x 42"	3	3½" squares
Fabric E Sails ⅛ yard each of two fabrics	1*	4" x 42"	2*	4" squares
		*cut for each fabric	2*	3½" squares
Frog Block and Row				
Fabric A Background ⅝ yard**	3	2½" x 42"	12	2½" x 8½"
	2	2" x 42"	5	2" x 9½"
	2	1½" x 42"	12	1½" x 4½"
			6	1½" squares
	1	1¼" x 42"	2	1¼" x 9½"
	1	1" x 42"	6	1" x 3½"
Fabric B Body ¼ yard each of two fabrics	1*	3" x 42"	3*	3" x 3½"
	2*	1½" x 42"	6*	1½" x 5½"
		*cut for each fabric	6*	1½" x 2½"
			6*	1½" squares
Fabric C Chest ⅛ yard each of two fabrics	1*	3½" x 42"	3*	3½" x 5½"
		*cut for each fabric		
Snake Row				
Fabric A Background ½ yard**	4	3½" x 42"	1	3½" x 9"
			39	3½" squares
Fabric B Snake Top ¼ yard	2	3½" x 42"	10	3½" x 6½"
Fabric C Snake Bottom ¼ yard	2	3½" x 42"	8	3½" x 6½"
Pinwheel Block and Row				
Fabric A Background ⅜ yard**	2	5½" x 42"	14	5½" squares
Fabric B Pinwheels ¼ yard each of seven fabrics	1*	5½" x 42"	2*	5½" squares
		*cut for each fabric		

Snips & Snails Row Quilt CONTINUED	FIRST CUT		SECOND CUT	
	Number of Strips or Pieces	Dimensions	Number of Pieces	Dimensions
Snail Block and Row				
Fabric A Background ⅝ yard**	1	2½" x 42"	6	2½" x 6½"
	2	2" x 42"	5	2" x 9½"
	5	1½" x 42"	6	1½" x 7½"
			6	1½" x 6½"
			6	1½" x 2½"
			30	1½" squares
	1	1¼" x 42"	2	1¼" x 9½"
Fabric B Body ¼ yard	4	1½" x 42"	6	1½" x 8½"
			6	1½" x 7½"
			6	1½" x 2½"
			6	1½" squares
Fabric C Shell ¼ yard each of three fabrics	2*	6½" square *cut for each fabric		
Checkerboard Block and Row				
Fabric A Light Squares ½ yard	4	3½" x 42"		
Fabric B Medium Squares ¼ yard	2	3½" x 42"		
Fabric C Dark Squares ¼ yard	2	3½" x 42"		
Accent Strips and Borders				
First Accent Strip Repeating Stripe 1⅞ yards***	1	63½" x 5½"		
	2	63½" x 4½"		
	1	63½" x 3½"		
	2	63½" x 1½"		
Second Accent Strip ½ yard	9	1½" x 42"		
Third Accent Strip ¼ yard	2	2½" x 42"		
Fourth Accent Strip ¼ yard	2	3½" x 42"		
Fifth Accent Strip ⅛ yard	2	1½" x 42"		
First Border ⅓ yard	8	1" x 42"		
Outside Border ⅔ yard	8	2½" x 42"		
Binding ⅞ yard	9	2¾" x 42"		

Backing - 5½ yards
Batting - 77" x 98"
** If using one fabric for Fabric A, total yardage needed is 2⅓ yards
***If using repeating stripe fabric adjust yardage to obtain the appropriate number of strips. Cut strips were cut lengthwise (parallel to salvage.)

Fabric Requirements and Cutting Instructions

Read all instructions before beginning and use ¼"-wide seam allowances throughout. Read Cutting Strips and Pieces on page 92 prior to cutting fabric pieces.

Getting Started

Young boys love playing in dirt and water and bringing precious treasures home from their 'adventures'. These interests are highlighted in this quilt with frogs, snakes, snails, pinwheels, and sailboats. Blocks measures 9½" square (unfinished).The quilt uses a repeating stripe for color inspiration and use in accent strips. We used 6 different sections of various widths. Adjust your yardage if necessary. Refer to Accurate Seam Allowance on page 92. Whenever possible use Assembly Line Method on page 92. Press seams in the direction of arrows.

Making the Sailboat Block and Row

Our quilt uses two different fabrics for the boat hull and three different fabrics for the sails. To obtain a scrappier look, use an assortment of fabrics to make each block uniquely different.

1. Refer to Quick Corner Triangles on page 92. Making a quick corner triangle unit, sew one 3½" Fabric D piece to one 3½" x 6½" Fabric A piece as shown. Press.

Fabric D = 3½ x 3½
Fabric A = 3½ x 6½

SNIPS & SNAILS TWIN BED QUILT
Finished Size: 69" x 89"

All his favorite things march across this quilt row by row. Sailboats and silly snails, pinwheels and friendly frogs, even slithering rickrack snakes meet in the middle of this twin quilt. You'll love how easy it is to put this quilt together and how flexible it is for personalization.

2. Draw a diagonal line on wrong side of one 4" Fabric A square. Place marked square and one 4" Fabric D square right sides together. Sew scant ¼" away from drawn line on both sides to make half-square triangles as shown. Cut on drawn line and press. Square to 3½". This will make two half-square triangle units.

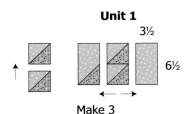

Fabric A = 4 x 4   Square to 3½
Fabric D = 4 x 4   Make 2
                Half-square Triangles

3. Sew two units from step 3 together as shown. Press. Sew this unit between unit from step 1 and one 3½" x 6½" Fabric A piece. Press and label Unit 1. Repeat steps 1-3 to make three of Unit 1.

Unit 1

3½

6½

Make 3

4. Repeat steps 1-3 to make four of Unit 1, using Fabric E fabrics. Make two of each combination.

Unit 1   **Unit 1**

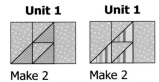

Make 2   Make 2

SNIPS & SNAILS TWIN BED QUILT Finished Size: 69" x 89"

5. Making quick corner triangle units, sew two 3½" Fabric A squares to one 3½" x 9½" Fabric C piece as shown to make Unit 2. Press. Make four.

Unit 2

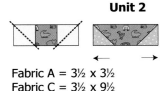

Fabric A = 3½ x 3½
Fabric C = 3½ x 9½
Make 4

6. Repeat step 5 to make three of Unit 2 using 3½" x 9½" Fabric B pieces.

Unit 2

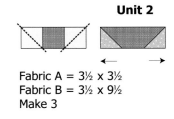

Fabric A = 3½ x 3½
Fabric B = 3½ x 9½
Make 3

7. Sew one Unit 1 to one Unit 2 as shown. Press. Make seven, each using a different combination of fabrics. Block measures 9½" square. Press last seam opposite from block to block for easier row construction.

Make 7
(each using a different combination of fabrics)
Block measures 9 ½" square.

8. Arrange and sew seven blocks together as shown. Press. Sailboat Row measures 9½" x 63½".

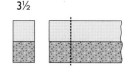

Row measures 9½" x 63½"

Making the Checkerboard Block and Row

1. Sew together lengthwise one 3½" x 42" Fabric A strip and one 3½" x 42" Fabric B strip to make a strip set. Press seams toward Fabric A. Make two. Cut strip set into twenty-one 3½"-wide segments as shown.

3½

Make 2
Cut 21 segments

2. Sew together lengthwise one 3½" x 42" Fabric A strip and one 3½" x 42" Fabric C strip to make a strip set. Press seams toward Fabric A. Make two. Cut strip set into twenty-one 3½"-wide segments, as shown.

3½

Make 2
Cut 21 segments

3. Sew two segments from step 1 together as shown. Press. Make four and label Unit 1. Sew one segment from step 2 and one segment from step 1 as shown. Press. Make twelve and label Unit 2. Sew two segments from step 2 together as shown. Press. Make four and label Unit 3.

Unit 1   **Unit 2**   **Unit 3**

Make 4   Make 12   Make 4

4. Arrange and sew three of Unit 1, five of Unit 2, two of Unit 3, and one segment from step 2 as shown. Press. Checkerboard Row 1 measures 6½" x 63½".

Row measures 6½" x 63½"

5. Arrange and sew two of Unit 3, seven of Unit 2, one Unit 1, and one segment from step 1 as shown. Press and label Row 6. Checkerboard Row 2 measures 6½" x 63½".

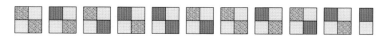

Row measures 6½" x 63½"

Making the Frog Block and Row

1. Refer to Snips and Snails Wall Quilt to make Frog Block steps 1-7 on pages 73, 74, and 77. Make six, three of each combination.

2. Arrange and sew together two 1¼" x 9½" Fabric A pieces, six Frog Blocks, and five 2" x 9½" Fabric A pieces as shown. Press. Frog Row measures 9½" x 63½".

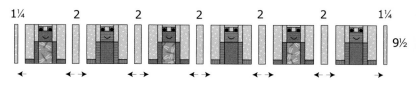

Row measures 9½" x 63½"

Making the Snake Row

1. Refer to Quick Corner Triangles on page 92. Making quick corner triangle units, sew two 3½" Fabric A squares to one 3½" x 6½" Fabric B piece as shown. Press. Make ten. Arrange and sew five units together as shown. Press. Make two.

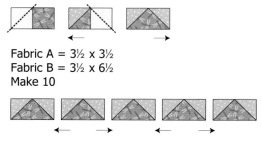

Fabric A = 3½ x 3½
Fabric B = 3½ x 6½
Make 10

Make 2

2. Making quick corner triangle units, sew two 3½" Fabric A squares to one 3½" x 6½" Fabric C piece as shown. Press. Make eight. Arrange and sew four units together as shown. Press. Make two.

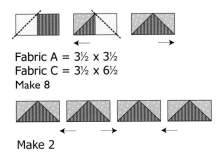

Fabric A = 3½ x 3½
Fabric C = 3½ x 6½
Make 8

Make 2

3. Sew one 3½" Fabric A square between two units from step 1 as shown. Press.

3½

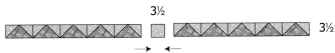

3½

4. Arrange and sew together two 3½" Fabric A squares, two units from step 2, and one 3½" x 9½" Fabric A piece as shown. Press.

3½   9½   3½

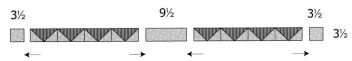

3½

5. Sew unit from step 3 to unit from step 4 together as shown, checking orientation of units prior to sewing. Press. Snake Row measures 6½" x 63½".

3½

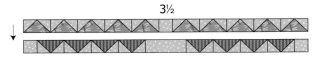

Row measures 6½" x 63½"

6. Refer to appliqué instructions on page 93, eye template below and photo on page 79 to position and fuse eye appliqués to snakes. Finish appliqué edges with machine satin stitch or other decorative stitching as desired.

Snips & Snails Twin Bed Quilt

Tracing Line _____

Snake Eye

Making the Pinwheel Block and Row

1. Draw a diagonal line on wrong side of one 5½" Fabric A square. Place marked square and one 5½" Fabric B square right sides together. Sew scant ¼" away from drawn line on both sides to make half-square triangles as shown. Make fourteen, two of each combination. Cut on drawn line and press. Square to 5". This will make twenty-eight half-square triangle units, four of each combination.

Fabric A = 5½ x 5½   Square to 5
Fabric C = 5½ x 5½   Make 28
Make 14   Half-square Triangles
(2 of each combination) (4 of each combination)

2. Sew two units from step 1 together as shown. Press. Make fourteen. Sew pairs together. Refer to Twisting Seams on page 92. Press. Make seven, in different fabric combinations.

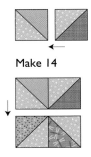

Make 14

Make 7
(in different combinations)

3. Arrange and sew together seven blocks from step 2. Press. Pinwheel Row measures 9½" x 63½".

Row measures 9½" x 63½"

Making the Snail Block and Row

1. Refer to Snips and Snails Wall Quilt to make Snail Block steps 1-10 on pages 74-76. Make six, two of each combination.

2. Arrange and sew together two 1¼" x 9½" Fabric A pieces, six Snail Blocks, and five 2" x 9½" Fabric A pieces as shown. Press. Snail Row measures 9½" x 63½".

1¼   2   2   2   2   2   1¼

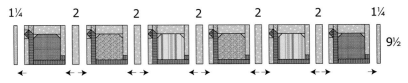

9½

Row measures 9½" x 63½"

Assembling the Quilt

1. Sew 1½" x 42" Second Accent strips together end-to-end to make one continuous 1½"-wide Second Accent strip. Press. Cut five 1½" x 63½" Second Accent strips.

2. Sew 2½" x 42" Third Accent strips together end-to-end to make one continuous 2½"-wide Third Accent strip. Press. Cut one 2½" x 63½" Third Accent strip.

3. Repeat step 2 to sew 2½"-wide Fourth Accent strips and 1½"-wide Fifth Accent strips, end-to-end and cut each into 63½" strips.

4. Refer to photo on page 79 and layout on page 81, arrange and sew together, 4½"-wide First Accent strip, Sailboat Row, one 1½"-wide Second Accent strip, Checkerboard Row 1, 1½"-wide Second Accent strip, Frog Row, 2½"-wide Third Accent strip, 3½"-wide First Accent strip, 1½"-wide Second Accent strip, Snake Row, 1½"-wide Second Accent strip, 5½"-wide First Accent strip, 1½"-wide First Accent Border, Pinwheel Row, 1½"-wide First Accent strip, 3½"-wide Fourth Accent strip, Checkerboard Row 2, 1½"-wide Fifth Accent strip, 1½"-wide Second Accent strip, Snail Row, and 4½"-wide First Accent strip. Press.

5. Refer to Adding the Borders on page 94. Sew 1" x 42" First Border strips together end-to-end to make one continuous 1"-wide strip. Measure quilt through center from side to side. Cut two 1"-wide First Border strips to this measurement. Sew to top and bottom of quilt. Press seams toward border.

6. Measure quilt through center from top to bottom including borders just added. Cut two 1"-wide First Border strips to this measurement. Sew to sides of quilt. Press.

7. Refer to steps 1 and 2 to join, measure, trim, and sew 2½"-wide Outside Border strips to top, bottom, and sides of quilt. Press.

Layering and Finishing

1. Cut backing crosswise into two equal pieces. Sew pieces together lengthwise to make one 98" x 80" (approximate) backing piece.

2. Referring to Layering the Quilt on page 94, arrange and baste backing, batting, and top together. Hand or machine quilt as desired.

3. Sew 2¾" x 42" binding strips end-to-end to make one continuous 2¾"-wide binding strip. Refer to Binding the Quilt on page 94 and bind quilt to finish.

Snips & Snails
DRAWER PULLS

Dress up a plain dresser or night stand with colorful, boy-friendly, drawer pulls.

1. Paint knobs in your choice of colors. Two or more coats of paint may be needed for good coverage. Allow to dry completely after each coat.

2. Select a character from scrapbook paper to feature on each knob. Using circle template, draw a circle around each character making sure to center character. Cut out circles using a scallop-edge scissors, cutting inside the drawn line.

3. Apply decoupage to top of one knob, then smooth prepared scrapbook paper circle onto knob, holding edges until they adhere. Cover entire knob with decoupage, allow to dry. Apply two or more additional coats of decoupage. Repeat for each knob.

4. When knobs are completely dry, secure to dresser.

SUPPLIES

1¾" Wood Drawer Pulls
Acrylic Craft Paints in Colors of Your Choice
Assorted Paintbrushes
Scrapbook Paper with Bugs, Frogs, etc.
1¾" Circle Template
Scallop-Edge Scissors
Gloss Decoupage

Making the Valance

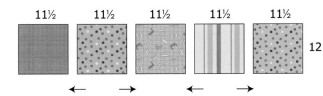

1. Arrange and sew together five different 11½" x 12" Fabric A pieces as shown. Press.

11½	11½	11½	11½	11½
				12

← → ← →

Snips & Snails Valance Finished Size: 15½" x 55"	FIRST CUT	
	Number of Strips or Pieces	Dimensions
Fabric A Panels ⅜ yard each of five fabrics	1*	11½" x 12" *cut for each fabric
Fabric B Accent ⅛ yard	2	1" x 42"
Fabric C Bottom Border ⅓ yard	2	4½" x 42"
Fabric D Tabs ⅛ yard assorted scraps cut from six fabrics	9** 2**	6½" x 4½" 3½" x 4½" **cut from assorted fabrics
Lining 1 yard	2	15¾" x 42"

2. Fold lengthwise one 6½" x 4½" Fabric D piece right sides together. Sew using ¼"-wide seam along 6½" side. Turn right side out. Press, placing seam in center back. Make nine from assorted scraps.

3. Repeat step 2 to sew one 3½" x 4½" Fabric D piece lengthwise, right sides together, along 3½" side. Turn right side out. Press. Make two in assorted scraps.

4. Referring to photo and step 6 diagram, arrange tabs across top of unit from step 1, placing the tabs from step 3, ¼" from each end to allow for seam allowance. Baste in place.

5. Sew 1" x 42" Fabric B strips together end-to-end to make one continuous 1"-wide Fabric B strip. Press. Repeat step to sew 4½"-wide Fabric C strip. Press. Sew strips together lengthwise staggering seams. Press seam toward Fabric C. Measure and cut strip set to measure 55½".

6. Sew unit from step 4 to unit from step 5 as shown. Press.

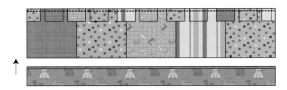

Fabric Requirements and Cutting Instructions

Read all instructions before beginning and use ¼"-wide seam allowances throughout. Read Cutting Strips and Pieces on page 92 prior to cutting fabric.

Getting Started

Add that touch of fun to a child's room with this easy to make valance. Refer to Accurate Seam Allowance on page 92. Press seams in the direction of arrows.

7. Sew 15¾" x 42" Lining strips together end-to-end to make one continuous 15¾"-wide strip. Press. Cut strip to measure 55½". The lining is cut shorter than the valance front so that the bottom seam will be drawn to and visible only from the back.

8. Place lining and valance right sides together. Sew top and bottom edges. Turn right side out and press, making sure that ¼" bottom seam is even and visible only from the back.

9. Turn right sides together and stitch side seams. (Bottom is folded along pressing line and hem seam is ¼" away from fold. Sew one side edge being careful not to catch tab in seam. Repeat for other side but leave a 5" opening for turning. Clip corners, turn right side out, and press. Hand-stitch opening closed.

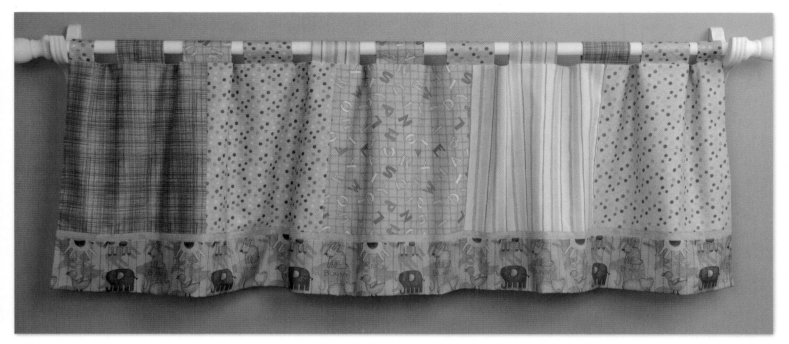

SNIPS & SNAILS WINDOW VALANCE

Finished Size: 15½" x 55"

Finish his cute room with a coordinating valance for his window. A mix of fabric colors and patterns draws the eye to this winsome window treatment.

Polka Dot **PEGS**

Encourage your little fellow to hang up his hats with these cute polka dot pegs. The pegs make a cute room decoration by repeating the colors and dot motifs in the valance and quilts.

1. Refer to General Painting Directions on page 95. Apply Gesso to pegs and allow to dry thoroughly. Gesso raises the grain, so sand pegs until smooth and remove residue with damp cloth.

2. Paint circles and pegs making one orange, one yellow, and one blue. Two or more coats of paint may be needed for good coverage. Allow paint to dry thoroughly after each coat.

3. Paint knobs on pegs, using a contrasting color as shown in photo. Allow to dry.

4. Following manufacturer's directions, apply several coats of gloss varnish. Hang on wall as desired.

Three Wood Circle Peg Hooks

Gesso

Fine Sandpaper

Acrylic Craft Paints — Americana® Moon Yellow and Jack-o'-lantern Orange; FolkArt® True Blue

Gloss Varnish

Assorted Paintbrushes

FROG PILLOW

Frog Pillow Finished Size: 21½" x 21½"	FIRST CUT	
	Number of Strips or Pieces	Dimensions
Fabric A Center ½ yard	1	13½" square
Fabric B Accent Border ⅛ yard	2 2	1¼" x 15" 1¼" x 13½"
Fabric C Outside Border ⅓ yard	2 2	4" x 22" 4" x 15"
Backing ⅔ yard	2	22" x 13¾"

Lining - ⅔ yard
Frog Appliqué - ⅓ yard
Batting - 24" x 24"
Lightweight Fusible Web - ⅓ yard
Pillow Form - 13" or 21½"
Pillow Form Fabric - ½ yard or ⅔ yard (Optional)
    Two 13½" squares or Two 22" squares
Polyester Fiberfill (Optional)

Adding the Appliqués

Refer to appliqué instructions on page 93. Our instructions are for Quick-Fuse Appliqué, but if you prefer hand appliqué, reverse templates and add ¼"-wide seam allowance.

1. Use patterns on pages 87 and 88 to trace frog on paper side of fusible web. Use appropriate fabrics to prepare all appliqués for fusing.

2. Refer to photo to position and fuse appliqués to 13½" Fabric A square. Finish appliqué edges with machine satin stitch or other decorative stitching as desired. Transfer mouth placement to frog head. Hand or machine satin stitch, as desired.

Finishing the Pillow

1. Sew appliqué frog square between two 1¼" x 13½" Fabric B strips. Press seams toward Fabric B. Sew this unit between two 1¼" x 15" Fabric B strips. Press.

2. Sew unit from step 1 between two 4" x 15" Fabric C strips. Press seams toward Fabric C. Sew this unit between two 4" x 22" Fabric C strips. Press.

3. Referring to Finishing Pillows on page 95, step 1, to prepare pillow top for quilting. Quilt as desired.

4. Use two 13¾" x 22" backing pieces and refer to Finishing Pillows, page 95, steps 2-4, to sew backing. Note: If a smaller pillow with flange is desired stitch in the ditch between center and accent border. Insert 21½" or 13" pillow form or refer to Pillow Forms page 95 to make a pillow form.

Rrribbit! A friendly speckled frog will greet him each morning when you add this playful pillow to his bed ensemble. Quick-Fuse appliqué makes this project fast and fun.

FROG PILLOW
Finished Size: 21½" x 21½"

Frog Pillow

Tracing Line ——————————
Placement Line ·—·—·—·—·—·—·—

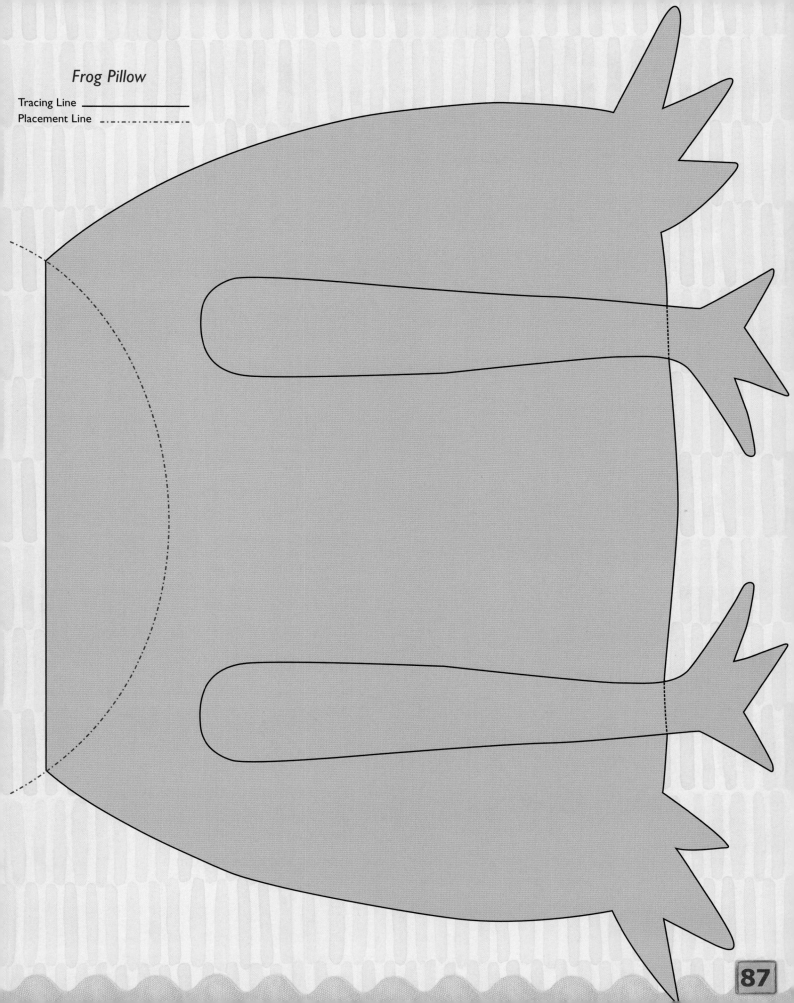

Frog Pillow

Tracing Line ———————
Embroidery Placement ·················

Collector JARS

These cute jars are perfect for nursery essentials then grow into a great place for a little guy to stash his favorite collectibles. Whether used for rocks, cars, or cotton balls, these jars are both functional and decorative. Scrapbook stickers make it easy to create jars to perfectly match bedroom décor

1. If you want to change the color of the lids, spray with primer and allow to dry.

2. Apply acrylic craft paints in your choice of colors. Two or more coats may be needed for good coverage. Allow to dry thoroughly after each coat.

3. Following manufacturer's directions, spray lids with matte or gloss varnish to protect paint.

4. Using our jars as inspiration, affix ribbons, scrapbook papers, and stickers to jars.

5. Adhere ribbon to lids using craft glue.

Jars with decorative lids

Spray Primer (Optional)

Acrylic Craft Paints in your choice of colors (Optional)

Spray Varnish (Optional)

Assorted Paintbrushes

Assorted Ribbons; Craft Glue

Scrapbook Paper & Stickers

Frog
WALL ART

This happy fellow grins with delight as he watches little boys play. Use the same appliqué pattern as the pillow to make this wall plaque.

1. Refer to General Painting Directions on page 95. Apply Gesso to wood plaque to prepare surface for painting. When thoroughly dry, lightly sand plaque until surface is smooth and remove residue with damp cloth.

2. Paint top side of plaque with a color that will accentuate appliqué fabric. We used Copen Blue mixed with a small amount of white paint. Two or more coats of paint may be needed for good coverage. Paint sides of plaque a darker shade of plaque color; we used True Blue. Allow to dry thoroughly.

3. Paint discs in complementary or contrasting colors. We painted three True Blue, two Moon Yellow, and two Jack-o'-lantern Orange.

4. Prepare appliqués following directions for Quick-Fuse Appliqué on page 93. Use a wide satin stitch to make frog mouth. Determine placement and fuse appliqués directly to board.

5. Glue painted discs at bottom of plaque and glue rickrack above discs. Spray plaque with Satin Varnish and allow to dry.

6. Thread brown thread through buttons and glue to frog appliqué for eyes.

7. Rickrack hanger is decorative only. Referring to photo, glue two strands of rickrack to back of plaque. Drill small holes through one blue disc to line up with yellow and orange buttons. Using floss, sew disc, yellow, and orange buttons together. Hang plaque on wall using a sawtooth picture hanger. Pin rickrack hanger and button embellishment to wall, going through button holes.

SUPPLIES

11" x 14" Wood Plaque Board

Gesso; Fine Sandpaper

Acrylic Craft Paints — Americana® Moon Yellow and Jack-o'-lantern Orange; FolkArt® True Blue; Delta Ceramcoat® Copen Blue; White

Matte Varnish; Assorted Paintbrushes

Green Rickrack

Seven 1½" Wood Discs

Three ¾" Yellow Buttons

One ⅜" Orange Button

Applique Fabric — ⅓ Yard

Fusible Web — ⅓ Yard

Craft Glue; Spray Satin Varnish

Sawtooth Picture Hanger

CUTE CRITTERS
WALL ART

Hop, hop, shuffle...Create cute critters for a little boy to enjoy as they add color and style to his fun-loving room. These wall plaques don't require a lot of time or painting skill and add the perfect finishing touch to a little boy's haven.

SUPPLIES

Eight 12" Stretcher Bars
(Available at art supply or craft store)

Four 18" Squares of Quilting Fabric
(Fabric is doubled for stability*)

Staple Gun and Staples

Frog Wood Cut-Out
(Measures 5½" x 5" approximately)

Turtle Wood Cut-Out
(Measures 7" x 4" approximately)

⅜"-wide Orange Ribbon — 2½ yards;
Cut into eight 11" pieces

Acrylic Craft Paints — Delta Ceramcoat®
Leaf Green, Wedgwood Blue, and Poppy Orange;
Americana® Moon Yellow;
FolkArt® Hauser Green Light and True Blue;
Black, and White

Assorted Paint Brushes

Gesso

Fabric Glue

Fine Sandpaper

Matte Varnish

Eight ¾" Green Buttons

Yellow Embroidery Floss

Assorted Buttons as Desired

Tacky Glue

Picture or Sawtooth Hangers

*If using heavyweight fabric, two 18" pieces will suffice.

Painting the Frog and Turtle

1. Refer to General Painting Directions on page 95.

2. Apply Gesso to wood cut-outs to prepare wood for finishing. When completely dry, sand lightly and remove residue with damp cloth.

3. Paint Frog (except dots and eyes) with Hauser Green Light. Two or more coats of paint may be needed for good coverage. Allow cut-out to dry completely after each coat.

4. Paint turtle head, legs, and tail with Hauser Green Light. Paint shell (except raised details) with Moon Yellow. Two or more coats of paint may be needed for good coverage. Allow to dry completely after each coat.

5. Using a dry brush technique and Leaf Green paint, add texture to Hauser Green Light areas. To dry brush, dip brush into Leaf Green paint, then blot several times on paper towel until just a little paint remains in brush. "Scrub" paint onto green areas. Continue until desired color and texture is achieved. Allow to dry completely.

6. Paint raised dots on frog and raised squares on turtle with colors as desired. Allow to dry.

7. Paint black circles for frog eyes adding a small white dot at the corner of eye as shown. Paint eye on turtle as shown.

8. When completely dry, apply matte varnish to cut-outs.

Preparing the Fabric Backgrounds

1. Slide interlocking stretcher bars together. Check for square by measuring from corner to corner, repeat for other side, and adjust if necessary. Staple at corners.

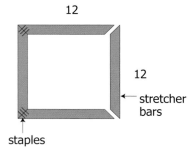

12

12

stretcher bars

staples

CUTE CRITTERS WALL ART
Finished Size: 12" x 12"

2. Because quilting fabric is lightweight, use two 18" pieces of fabric for each wall piece. Place the two 18" squares right side down under bar unit from step 1. Pull fabric around bar, staple in the middle of each stretcher bar, pulling fabric tightly to obtain good tension. Continue process, working from center, stretching and stapling fabric, stopping at corners.

Back View

3. Pull corner tight and check front to make sure fabric is taut. Fold excess fabric at 90°, crease, and form corner. Staple tightly to back.

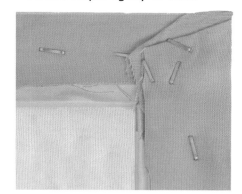

4. If desired attach a wire picture hanger or sawtooth hanger to back of each fabric wall piece.

5. Using fabric glue and a ruler as a placement guide, glue ribbon 1¼" from edges on each fabric background, intersecting at corners as shown in photo. Thread yellow floss through green buttons and tie on top. Glue buttons at intersections of ribbon.

6. Since the turtle cutout doesn't have the same "weight" as the frog, a decorative element is added to the turtle wall piece. Cut one 2" x 6¾" strip from one of the fabrcis used in the quilt. Fold under all edges ¼" to the wrong side. Press and edgestitch or add decorative stitching to hold folded edge in place. Center and glue strip to wall piece placing it ⅞ " above bottom ribbon.

7. Use tacky glue to glue frog and turtle cut-outs to each prepared background. Allow to dry thoroughly.

GENERAL DIRECTIONS

Cutting Strips and Pieces

We recommend washing cotton fabrics in cold water and pressing before making projects in this book. Using a rotary cutter, see-through ruler, and a cutting mat, cut the strips and pieces for the project. If indicated on the Cutting Chart, some will need to be cut again into smaller strips and pieces. Make second cuts in order shown to maximize use of fabric. The yardage amounts and cutting instructions are based on an approximate fabric width of 42".

Pressing

Pressing is very important for accurate seam allowances. Press seams using either steam or dry heat with an "up and down" motion. Do not use side-to-side motion as this will distort the unit or block. Set the seam by pressing along the line of stitching, then press seams to one side as indicated by project instructions and diagram arrows.

Twisting Seams

When a block has several seams meeting in the center as shown, there will be less bulk if seam allowances are pressed in a circular type direction and the center intersection "twisted". Remove 1-2 stitches in the seam allowance to enable the center to twist and lay flat. This technique aids in quilt assembly by allowing the seams to fall opposite each other when repeated blocks are next to each other. The technique works well with 4-patch blocks, pinwheel blocks, and quarter-square triangle blocks.

Accurate Seam Allowance

Accurate seam allowances are always important, but especially when the blocks contain many pieces and the quilt top contains multiple pieced borders. If each seam is off as little as 1/16", you'll soon find yourself struggling with components that just won't fit.

To ensure seams are a perfect 1/4"-wide, try this simple test: Cut three strips of fabric, each exactly 1½" x 12". With right sides together, and long raw edges aligned, sew two strips together, carefully maintaining a 1/4" seam. Press seam to one side. Add the third strip to complete the strip set. Press and measure. The finished strip set should measure 3½" x 12". The center strip should measure 1"-wide, the two outside strips 1¼"-wide, and the seam allowances exactly 1/4".

If your measurements differ, check to make sure that seams have been pressed flat. If strip set still doesn't "measure up," try stitching a new strip set, adjusting the seam allowance until a perfect 1/4"-wide seam is achieve.

Assembly Line Method

Whenever possible, use an assembly line method. Position pieces right sides together and line up next to sewing machine. Stitch first unit together, then continue sewing others without breaking threads. When all units are sewn, clip threads to separate. Press seams in direction of arrows as shown in step-by-step project diagrams.

Quick Corner Triangles

Quick corner triangles are formed by simply sewing fabric squares to other squares or rectangles. The directions and diagrams with each project illustrate what size pieces to use and where to place squares on the corresponding piece. Follow steps 1–3 below to make quick corner triangle units.

1. With pencil and ruler, draw diagonal line on wrong side of fabric square that will form the triangle. This will be your sewing line.

   Sewing line

2. With right sides together, place square on corresponding piece. Matching raw edges, pin in place, and sew ON drawn line. Trim off excess fabric, leaving 1/4"-wide seam allowance as shown.

   Trim 1/4" away from sewing line

3. Press seam in direction of arrow as shown in step-by-step project diagram. Measure completed quick corner triangle unit to ensure the greatest accuracy.

   Finished quick corner triangle unit

Fussy Cut

To make a "fussy cut," carefully position ruler or template over a selected design in fabric. Include seam allowances before cutting desired pieces.

Quick-Fuse Appliqué

Quick-fuse appliqué is a method of adhering appliqué pieces to a background with fusible web. For quick and easy results, simply quick-fuse appliqué pieces in place. Use sewable, lightweight fusible web for the projects in this book unless otherwise indicated. Finish raw edges with stitching as desired. Laundering is not recommended unless edges are finished.

1. With paper side up, lay fusible web over appliqué pattern. Leaving ½" space between pieces, trace all elements of design. Cut around traced pieces, approximately ¼" outside traced line.

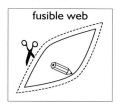

fusible web

2. With paper side up, position and press fusible web to wrong side of selected fabrics. Follow manufacturer's directions for iron temperature and fusing time. Cut out each piece on traced line.

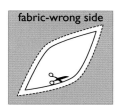

fabric-wrong side

3. Remove paper backing from pieces. A thin film will remain on wrong side of fabric. Position and fuse all pieces of one appliqué design at a time onto background, referring to photos for placement. Fused design will be the reverse of traced pattern.

Appliqué Pressing Sheet

An appliqué pressing sheet is very helpful when there are many small elements to apply using a quick-fuse appliqué technique. The pressing sheet allows small items to be bonded together before applying them to the background. The sheet is coated with a special material that prevents fusible web from adhering permanently to the sheet. Follow manufacturer's directions. Remember to let fabric cool completely before lifting it from the appliqué sheet. If not cooled, the fusible web could remain on the sheet instead of on the fabric.

Machine Appliqué

This technique should be used when you are planning to launder quick-fuse projects. Several different stitches can be used: small narrow zigzag stitch, satin stitch, blanket stitch, or another decorative machine stitch. Use an open toe appliqué foot if your machine has one. Use a stabilizer to obtain even stitches and help prevent puckering. Always practice first to check machine settings.

1. Fuse all pieces following Quick-Fuse Appliqué directions.

2. Cut a piece of stabilizer large enough to extend beyond the area to be stitched. Pin to the wrong side of fabric.

3. Select thread to match appliqué.

4. Following the order that appliqués were positioned, stitch along the edges of each section. Anchor beginning and ending stitches by tying off or stitching in place two or three times.

5. Complete all stitching, then remove stabilizer.

Hand Appliqué

Hand appliqué is easy when you start out with the right supplies. Cotton and machine embroidery thread are easy to work with. Pick a color that matches the appliqué fabric as closely as possible. Use appliqué or silk pins for holding shapes in place and a long, thin needle, such as a sharp, for stitching.

1. Make a template for every shape in the appliqué design. Use a dotted line to show where pieces overlap.

2. Place template on right side of appliqué fabric. Trace around template.

3. Cut out shapes ¼" beyond traced line.

4. Position shapes on background fabric, referring to quilt layout. Pin shapes in place.

5. When layering and stitching appliqué shapes, always work from background to foreground. Where shapes overlap, do not turn under and stitch edges of bottom pieces. Turn and stitch the edges of the piece on top.

6. Use the traced line as your turn-under guide. Entering from the wrong side of the appliqué shape, bring the needle up on the traced line. Using the tip of the needle, turn under the fabric along the traced line. Using blind stitch, stitch along folded edge to join the appliqué shape to the background fabric. Turn under and stitch about ¼" at a time.

Adding the Borders

1. Measure quilt through the center from side to side. Trim two border strips to this measurement. Sew to top and bottom of quilt. Press seams toward border.

2. Measure quilt through the center from top to bottom, including borders added in step 1. Trim border strips to this measurement. Sew to sides and press. Repeat to add additional borders.

Layering the Quilt

1. Cut backing and batting 4" to 8" larger than quilt top.

2. Lay pressed backing on bottom (right side down), batting in middle, and pressed quilt top (right side up) on top. Make sure everything is centered and that backing and batting are flat. Backing and batting will extend beyond quilt top.

3. Begin basting in center and work toward outside edges. Baste vertically and horizontally, forming a 3"–4" grid. Baste or pin completely around edge of quilt top. Quilt as desired. Remove basting.

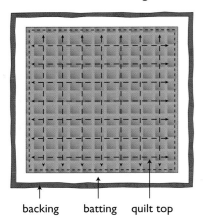

backing   batting   quilt top

Binding the Quilt

1. Trim batting and backing to ¼" beyond raw edge of quilt top. This will add fullness to binding.

2. Join binding strips to make one continuous strip if needed. To join, place strips perpendicular to each other, right sides together, and draw a diagonal line. Sew on drawn line and trim triangle extensions, leaving a ¼"-wide seam allowance. Continue stitching ends together to make the desired length. Press seams open.

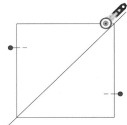
←trim

3. Fold and press binding strips in half lengthwise with wrong sides together.

4. Measure quilt through center from side to side. Cut two binding strips to this measurement. Lay binding strips on top and bottom edges of quilt top with raw edges of binding and quilt top aligned. Sew through all layers, ¼" from quilt edge. Press binding away from quilt top.

Front of Quilt

5. Measure quilt through center from top to bottom, including binding just added. Cut two binding strips to this measurement and sew to sides through all layers, including binding just added. Press.

6. Folding top and bottom first, fold binding around to back then repeat with sides. Press and pin in position. Hand-stitch binding in place using a blind stitch.

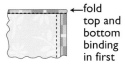
←fold top and bottom binding in first

Making Bias Strips

1. Refer to Fabric Requirements and Cutting Instructions for the amount of fabric required for the specific bias needed.

2. Remove selvages from the fabric piece and cut into a square. Mark edge with straight pin where selvages were removed as shown. Cut square once diagonally into two equal 45° triangles. (For larger squares, fold square in half diagonally and gently press fold. Open fabric square and cut on fold.)

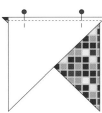

3. Place pinned edges right sides together and stitch along edge with a ¼" seam. Press seam open.

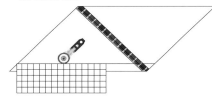

4. Using a ruler and rotary cutter, cut bias strips to width specified in quilt directions.

5. Each strip has a diagonal end. To join, place strips perpendicular to each other, right sides together, matching diagonal cut edges and allowing tips of angles to extend approximately ¼" beyond edges. Sew ¼"-wide seams. Continue stitching ends together to make the desired length. Press seams open. Cut strips into recommended lengths according to quilt directions.

Finishing Pillows

1. Layer batting between pillow top and lining. Baste. Hand or machine quilt as desired, unless otherwise indicated. Trim batting and lining even with raw edge of pillow top.

2. Narrow hem one long edge of each backing piece by folding under ¼" to wrong side. Press. Fold under ¼" again to wrong side. Press. Stitch along folded edge.

3. With right sides up, lay one backing piece over second piece so hemmed edges overlap, making backing unit the same measurement as the pillow top. Baste backing pieces together at top and bottom where they overlap.

4. With right sides together, position and pin pillow top to backing. Using ¼"-wide seam, sew around edges, trim corners, turn right side out, and press.

Pillow Forms

Cut two pieces of fabric to finished size of pillow form plus ½". Place right sides together, aligning raw edges. Using ¼"-wide seam, sew around all edges, leaving 5" opening for turning. Trim corners and turn right side out. Stuff to desired fullness with polyester fiberfill and hand-stitch opening closed.

Lacing Stitch

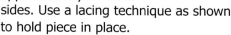

To insert a quilt block or piece of fabric inside a frame, wrap piece around mounting board with fabric extending approximately 2" on all sides. Use a lacing technique as shown to hold piece in place.

Couching Technique

Couching is a method of attaching a textured yarn, cord, or fiber to fabric for decorative purposes. Use an open-toe embroidery foot, couching foot, or a zigzag presser foot and matching or monofilament thread. Sew with a long zigzag stitch just barely wider than the cord or yarn. Stabilizer on the wrong side of fabric is recommended. Place the yarn, cord, or fiber on right side of fabric and zigzag to attach as shown. A hand-stitch can be used if desired.

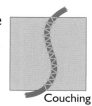

Couching

General Painting Directions

Read all instructions on paint products before using and carefully follow manufacturer's instructions and warnings. For best results, allow paint to dry thoroughly between each coat and between processes unless directed otherwise. Wear face mask and safety goggles when sanding. Rubber gloves are recommended when handling stains and other finishing products.

Dry Brush Technique

Dip dry brush in small amount of paint. Dab brush on paper towel until only a small amount of paint remains. Apply to surface to create a scratchy or textured effect.

Color Wash

Mix 3 parts of water to 1 part of paint. Load mixture on a large brush and apply a light, transparent coat of paint to surface.

Circle Templates

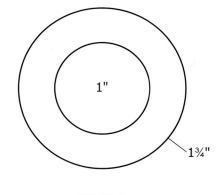

1"

1¾"

2¼"

2"

2¾"

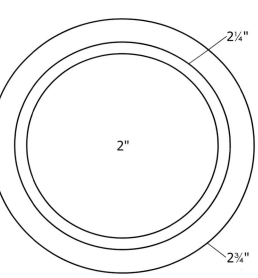

Embroidery Stitch Guide

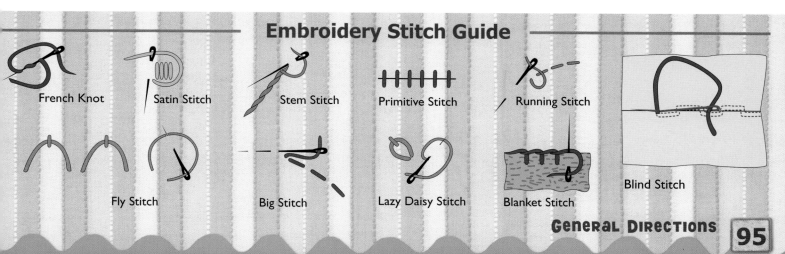

French Knot   Satin Stitch   Stem Stitch   Primitive Stitch   Running Stitch

Fly Stitch   Big Stitch   Lazy Daisy Stitch   Blanket Stitch   Blind Stitch

About Debbie Mumm

A talented designer, author, and entrepreneur, Debbie Mumm has been creating charming artwork and quilt designs for more than twenty years.

Debbie got her start in the quilting industry in 1986 with her unique and simple-to-construct quilt patterns. Since that time, she has authored more than fifty books featuring quilting and home decorating projects and has led her business to become a multi-faceted enterprise that includes publishing, fabric design, and licensed art divisions.

Known world-wide for the many licensed products that feature her designs, Debbie loves to bring traditional elements together with fresh palettes and modern themes to create the look of today's country.

Designs by Debbie Mumm
Special thanks to my creative teams:

Editorial & Project Design
Carolyn Ogden: Publications & Marketing Manager
Nancy Kirkland: Quilt Designer/Seamstress • Georgie Gerl: Technical Writer/Editor
Carolyn Lowe: Technical Editor • Jackie Saling: Craft Designer
Anita Pederson: Machine Quilter

Book Design & Production
Tom Harlow: Graphics Manager • Monica Ziegler: Graphic Designer
Kate Yates: Graphic Designer • Kris Clifford: Executive Assistant

Photography
Tom Harlow, Debbie Mumm® Graphics Studio

Children's Portraits
Dream Catcher Photography - www.dreamcatcherphotography.com
Special thanks to proud parents and Crystal Cooley of
Dream Catcher Photography for photos of the very cute kids.

Art Team
Kathy Arbuckle: Artist/Designer • Gil-Jin Foster: Artist

The Debbie Mumm® Sewing Studio exclusively uses Bernina® sewing machines.

©2008 Debbie Mumm

Produced by:
Debbie Mumm, Inc.
1116 E. Westview Court
Spokane, WA 99218
(509) 466-3572
Fax (509) 466-6919

www.debbiemumm.com

Published by:
Leisure Arts, Inc
5701 Ranch Drive
Little Rock, AR • 72223
www.leisurearts.com

Discover More from Debbie Mumm®

Debbie Mumm's®
Colors from Nature
96-page, soft cover

Joy Joy Joy
by Debbie Mumm®
96-page, soft cover

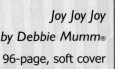

Debbie Mumm's®
Greenwood Gardens
96-page, soft cover

Debbie Mumm's®
New Expressions
96-page, soft cover

Available at local fabric
and craft shops or at
debbiemumm.com